LEAN INSIDE

7 STEPS TO PERSONAL POWER

A practical guide to transformation for women

JAY PRYOR

BALBOA.
PRESS

A DIVISION OF HAY HOUSE

Balboa Press books may be ordered through booksellers or by contacting:

Balboa Press
A Division of Hay House
1663 Liberty Drive
Bloomington, IN 47403
www.balboapress.com
1 (877) 407-4847

Because of the dynamic nature of the Internet, any web addresses or links contained in this book may have changed since publication and may no longer be valid. The views expressed in this work are solely those of the author and do not necessarily reflect the views of the publisher, and the publisher hereby disclaims any responsibility for them.

The author of this book does not dispense medical advice or prescribe the use of any technique as a form of treatment for physical, emotional, or medical problems without the advice of a physician, either directly or indirectly. The intent of the author is only to offer information of a general nature to help you in your quest for emotional and spiritual well-being. In the event you use any of the information in this book for yourself, which is your constitutional right, the author and the publisher assume no responsibility for your actions.

Any people depicted in stock imagery provided by Thinkstock are models, and such images are being used for illustrative purposes only. Certain stock imagery © Thinkstock.

Print information available on the last page.

ISBN: 978-1-5043-3947-6 (sc)
ISBN: 978-1-5043-3949-0 (hc)
ISBN: 978-1-5043-3948-3 (e)

Library of Congress Control Number: 2015916174

Balboa Press rev. date: 10/21/2015

CONTENTS

ACKNOWLEDGEMENT

I'm not kidding when I say this book could NOT have been written without my wife, best friend, and soul mate Jessica Crittenden Pryor. I tried to get her to share the by line, but she refused.

Jessica is the yin to my yang. Everything I do is better with her. When you read this book you get me filtered through her. She is a true blessing to the world. Thank you, Jessica, for helping me create this book and our life together. I am so blessed to have you as my wife, lover, best friend, playmate and work buddy.

Thanks also to my children Rose and Emmett who continue to be amazing children. You confront my SMALL and force me to constantly transform to be the kind of dad I want to be. Thanks for choosing me to be your Dad. I love you with all my heart.

Thanks to my family for always supporting what I am up to even when you don't really understand it.

Special thanks to my sister, Kathy, and brother, John, for reading and supporting my work. Also, thanks to them for admitting me to that psych ward 20 years ago. It saved my life and taught me so much. I know it was one of the hardest things you have ever done and you were young people doing it. You are my heroes and my champions.

Thanks to my friends and framily. I'm blessed to have a lot of them. You know who you are.

A special thank you to my early readers for the feedback and testimonials. They all couldn't fit on the back of the book, but I will cherish them always.

Thanks to all my mentors and coaches along the way and special thanks to my coach, Marie Jeanne Verhassel, for introducing me to the law of attraction and being my spiritual teacher; always reminding me that I am creating this dream and that we are one.

To the congregation of Dumbarton United Methodist Church for helping me reframe my stories around what church is and teaching me what a faith community can look like.

To the congregation at Unity Church of Lawrence for showing me what new thought principles are and how they work.

Extra special thanks to the Real Spiritual Entrepreneurs of Lawrence, your support and encouragement has me moving forward focused on what is working. You are my power posse. I can't imagine my life without you.

Finally a huge thank you to all the women of Lawrence, Kansas that have done my seminars, especially to the first 16 who took a leap of faith and allowed me the privilege of sharing this work. Thank you for showing me with your amazing sharing and vulnerability that this stuff works. You inspire me to no end the way you have come together to do the work and hold space for each other. The community you are building is so powerful. It blows my mind over and over again.

FOREWORD

I'd like to start this foreword with a "Thank ya, Jesus." Here's why.

I LOVE Jay Pryor with all my heart. He's part of my power posse. I've done his "Lean Inside" workshop. I consider him a close friend.

So I would have endorsed this book no matter what.

I'm so grateful that I can actually use one of Jay's principles ("Stay in integrity") and say with a straight face, "This is a damned good book."

In fact, I'm kinda mad. I've always loved Jay's talks. Pretty much everything that drops out of his mouth is inspiring, funny, and makes you want to be a better person. Because I, too, want to be an "inspiring speaker" and my B.S. (Belief System—you'll see, keep reading) tells me that I'm not quite there yet, I've always rationalized with "Well, Jay is a fabulous speaker, but I'm a fabulous writer." Now, I have to admit that "Jay is ALSO a fabulous writer." Damn it!

Not that I'm comparing or anything.

The main thing you need to know about Jay is he smokes what he sells. He doesn't just spout out a bunch of high-falutin' principles. He lives this stuff with his heart and soul. For that reason alone, you gotta read this book.

Thank you, Jay, for letting me do just that—before everybody else gets their grubby paws on it.

Like Jay, this book is real, it's inspiring and it has the power to transform lives.

–Pam Grout
#1 New York Times bestselling author of
E-Squared, E-Cubed, and 15 other books

WHO IS JAY PRYOR, AND WHY SHOULD I LISTEN TO HIM?

Lots of people have told me that I should share my story. Someday when Jodi Foster or Jenji Kohan ask me to write the screen play with them I will share it in detail. This book is designed to support you, to show you how you can transform your life and, with practice, wake up to a whole new level of happiness and productivity. I realize that it may help you to know that I have done the work myself, so here's the cliff notes version of my life story, and how I got from being a miserable, suicidal young woman to being a person who is thrilled with the path his life is on.

I was born in southeast Kansas in a town of 500 people. I am the youngest of nine kids, and in fact was the tie breaker. There were four girls and four boys in the family until I came along and broke the tie. I was a girl.

Throughout my childhood I consistently had the feeling that something was wrong with me. I couldn't put my finger on what, exactly, but I always knew that I was "different." I was always a tomboy, but so were my friends and other family members. That wasn't unusual.

However, when I turned about ten or eleven, my friends started wanting to wear make-up and to look pretty. That embarrassed me. I didn't understand why. I just knew that I hated it. It made me uncomfortable. I didn't protest for the most part. I just did what I had to do to get by. I put on dresses for church events, and was even in the show choir at school and wore a dress to every performance. It felt awkward, but I sucked it up to fit in and get by.

A girl kissed me when I was thirteen, and fireworks went off in my head. That was it! I figured out what was wrong. I was gay. For a brief moment I felt relieved. In the next moment I felt panic and loathing. I was someone who said things like, "I wouldn't walk across the street to piss on a queer if they were on fire." I once called a radio station to say that "all gay people should be shot." I was serious. This tells you the level of self-hatred that possessed me. I knew I couldn't tell anyone about this, so I didn't.

Something you should know about me is that I have always been a leader - or I had a big mouth, anyway. So the whole time that I hated my own guts and felt constantly suicidal, I was still very involved in my school activities. My junior year of high school, I was class president. And my senior year I was the student body president. My point in telling you that is to illustrate that even when people look like they are doing well by being a leader and participating in life, they can still hate themselves and hate their life.

My junior year of high school, I started trying to kill myself rather than just think about it. I had a few failed attempts that no one knew about. The first time I tried to overdose on diet pills and booze, but that just made me really sick. The second time, I drove my parents' car a hundred miles an hour down a country road. I headed for a culvert and pulled the steering wheel so I would flip. The car flipped end-over-end and landed jackknifed in a ditch on the opposite side of the road. I came out without a scratch. I told my parents I had swerved to miss a deer. After I graduated high school, I tried one more time to kill myself and my siblings found out about it.

They put me in a hospital. Yes, a psychiatric ward. I was eighteen years old and the youngest person on the adult ward. I was terrified. As it turned out, that would be one of the most significant events of my life. In the end I loved the experience. I know that sounds crazy (pun intended). I was safe and less stressed than I had been in years. I learned to love all people in that ward. At the young age of 18, I was handed a dose of humility that I desperately needed. I learned to get grateful. I was in that hospital for three weeks before I would talk to anyone. Finally they threatened to release me. That scared me worse than talking, so I started talking. I told them everything. For the first time in my life I said the words, "I am gay".

That hospital saved my life. I will be forever grateful to the staff of nurses and counselors that worked with me, as well as the other patients. That experience was the first time that I started to learn to *Lean Inside*. The counselors there introduced me to Amy Grant's music. That music touched my soul in a powerful way and got me grounded in my faith and reliance on God. That was the first time I really understood, or felt in some way that I was loved, and that I had a purpose. It put me on a path of personal transformation that started me on my journey to now.

It took a bit, but I eventually went to college and got my degree in Interpersonal and Organizational Communication Studies. Things were good, yet there was always something nagging at me having to do with how I was different. When I went back to college, for example, I grew my hair out and went back to being called by my birth name, Janet. I was trying to fit in and make it work.

In 1997 my friend Melanie sent me the book *Stone Butch Blues* by Leslie Feinberg. This book changed my life. I realized that I was not alone. There was a name for what I had been feeling: gender variant. Reading that book changed my perspective from feeling shame about being a butch, or masculine-gendered person, to experiencing pride in my difference. I found community online. Other women who did not fit into society's idea of what we should look and act like. Women who were attracted to butches and transmen. I went from feeling like an ugly woman to knowing myself as a handsome butch. I couldn't go back after that.

I decided to stop compromising. I believe this is when my transition started. I threw out all my girl clothes except my sports bras and I started going by the name Jay again. I had been called Jay when I was younger, but went back to Janet when I went back to college at the age of 24. I had it in my head that no one would take me seriously if I was going by a nickname, even though I loved it. The first woman to call me Jay was someone I had a crush on when I was a babe of 19. She was the most beautiful woman I had ever met. She called me "J" and then spelled my name "Jay" in a note she left me. When I saw it I thought my heart would burst. It was the first time I had a glimmer of what it felt to be truly known.

That spring my niece asked me to sing at her wedding. I told her I would love to sing, but that she would have to be okay with me doing it in a man's suit instead of a dress. Up until then, every time someone got married or died, I would be taken out by my mom or my sisters to buy a dress, since I didn't have one in my closet. My niece, Jennifer, and I have always been close. She didn't care what I wore, she just wanted me to sing.

That was the first time in my adult life that I went to a family event in my own clothes. I was 28 years old.

In 1999, I moved to Washington, DC where I met other transgender people. I resisted transitioning for a long time because I was afraid. I feared that my family would freak out and that I would lose my connection to the gay community. I loved being a part of the LGBT community. I didn't want the world to see me as a straight guy. Finally, in 2000 I saw a therapist and with her help I figured out that I did really want to change my body and face to be what truly matched my soul. I would just have to be "out" as a transgender person. So I did that.

At the age of 34, I took my first shot of testosterone on April 1st, 2001. I have been walking through the world as a man ever since.

After experiencing the world of "being a man," I still feel like part of me is woman and part of me is man. I look like a man on the outside, and I know that I was conditioned in the world to be a woman. I see the world from both perspectives. I almost exclusively coach executive women now, and part of what makes me a good coach for women is that I used to be one. I know how differently the world treats me as a man versus as a woman. To be honest, it pisses me off and grosses me out. It's part of why I serve women today, and have seminars exclusively for women. I empower women to know themselves as powerful and to create community with other women by building them up.

I mentioned that I started my personal development path at the age of 18 in a psych ward. From there, I continued to grow, change, and challenge myself to keep transforming anything and everything that might be in the way of my happiness. Right out of the hospital at 18, I did five years clean and sober in AA. Then I realized I wasn't an alcoholic, and moreover, I had been drinking a lot in high school to deal with being gay. Once I was out and didn't have to run from that, I didn't need to drink anymore. Still, learning the 12 steps of AA was a personal foundation for which I will always be grateful. In 2002, I did the Landmark Forum and all the Curriculum for Living through Landmark Education. In 2003, I was introduced to Abraham and started learning about The Law of Attraction. I started studying other coaches (Jack Canfield, Brian Tracy), I read all the old classics by Napoleon Hill, Zig Ziglar, and Stephen Covey. I loved this stuff and couldn't get enough.

In 2005, I went to coaching school and became a certified graduate of CoachU. I opened my own coaching practice in 2005, and began coaching people to fulfill their dreams, and to start their own journey of transformation. In 2007, I started attending a Unity church and was introduced to authors like Eric Butterworth, Florence Scovel Shinn, and Edwene Gaines. It became more and more obvious to me that all the great leaders of personal transformation were saying the same things. Happiness and fulfillment is an inside job. Learning to love and know that you are loved is key. Forgiveness is essential for you and for others. Learn to know and love your SELF.

That's my message, too. I know my purpose is to be another mouthpiece, yet another person sharing these principles. The meat of what you read in this book has been said before. Each person is called to hear it when they can hear it. You may hear it differently than I did.

Throughout the rest of this book, I will be operating under the assumption that you know that I am a two-spirited/gender queer/transsexual/former woman. I am out in my life. I am out so that I am comfortable. I'm out so that I can help other kids like me have it a little easier.

Thanks for reading the short version of my life journey. There are two key elements from all my experiences that build the basis of my work. The first is to Lean Inside: A connection to God/the Universe will support and heal me. Second is that what I say to myself makes all the difference in the world. Coming out of the psychiatric unit didn't stop the voices in my head that immediately went to thoughts of suicide any time something happened that scared me or was upsetting. Suicidal thoughts had become a habit. I made a decision around the age of 23 that I was no longer allowed to have those thoughts. It was a habit I had to break. I had to make it a matter of my own integrity that I would not let myself go to that place.

I know myself today as someone who is a powerful person. I know I am powerful, and I know that I am loved. I know that through loving my SELF I have an amazing life that I have consciously created, right down to my gender. I am so blessed to have this life. I hope you can glean something from my experience and the work that I do.

Namaste,

Jay Pryor

INTRODUCTION

This book is about transformation and training yourself as a human being or person.

The field I work in and love is the field of personal development, or spiritual development. We study being human and how to become more aware of how we function, physically and socially. The field of personal development involves spirituality, common sense, success principles, neuroscience, psychology, positive psychology, ontology, the law of attraction, quantum physics, emotional intelligence, spiritual intelligence, communication studies, mindfulness, wellness, morality, religion, and love.

Through all of these fields of study, and through all the different ways one can look at life, we have arrived at a few common points. This wisdom is shared in many personal development books and scriptural texts from every religious and spiritual practice. I encourage you to seek out the sources that speak to your heart and that support you in being the most powerful version of yourself.

My work is to assist you in the practical application of what the field of personal and spiritual development has to say about how much power we have over our experience of our lives. In other words, I didn't make this up, I'm just the nuts and bolts application guy. My role is to help you to see the patterns, beliefs, and limitations you create in your life, and know what to do to transform them. I want you to be awake to the power you have to make your life anything you can dream it could be.

This book breaks down some of this shared wisdom for you in a simple way, gives you actions you can take to start your own path, and guides you to further resources that will support you on your transformational journey.

Unlike other personal development leaders who may have it all together, I still have a way to go. And I'm committed to the journey. In writing this book, I will share my journey with you with the intention of supporting you during your own journey.

CHAPTER 1

The Purpose

The three purposes of this book are:

1. To start you on a path of personal transformation. My definition of transformation is chipping away at everything that is not your highest, best SELF by practicing progress not perfection.
2. To have you start to become conscious to, or awake to the fact that you create your own life through your thoughts, words, and energy, and for you to start doing it consciously, rather than by default.
3. My third, and most important purpose, is to have you know that you are loved and are worthy of love. People who know that they are loved behave in loving ways. People who know that they are loved are spiritually mature. They don't need to gossip or stir up trouble. They are secure in themselves. They see their impact on the world and have a commitment to make a difference.

Throughout my life I have seen people go from being people with no support or connection to their higher SELF turn into people who know they are loved. It is like watching a flower bloom. Just a little love and support for people goes a long way.

I want you to know that you are loved so that you can have real fulfillment and joy in your life. Being someone who is loved makes all that possible. I want a world full of people who know they are loved, who feel connected to the knowing that I have, which is the knowing of being loved.

CHAPTER 2

Waking Up!

All of my work comes from the premises that everything is energy, and we each create our own reality. I believe we do this through our thoughts, words, and emotions. If I could define my work in one question it would be, "Why are you creating it that way?" I ask my clients that question a lot. Anytime they tell me a story where they have a loss of power I ask them, "Why are you creating it that way?" I have clients with whom I have worked for years that are quite facile with using this perspective. This is how I look at my life. I own all of it. It is rare that I have times when life looks "real" to me. I feel blessed to have acquired that level of consciousness. There are still times when I get triggered, or hijacked, or I haven't managed my well-being. That is when life looks like it is happening to me. Fortunately, I have designed my life so that I am surrounded by people who can remind me that I am creating all of it and ask me the question, "Why are you creating it that way?" The answer usually is so that I can be right about something. It used to be so that I could be right about how unworthy I was. For the most part, that has disappeared for me. I know that I am loved beyond measure. Still, sometimes I find myself playing the victim or martyr. By doing so, I get to get out of being responsible, or I get to justify my bad behavior. It's always one of those things. Ego in charge.

When you can ask yourself, or look at, "Why am I creating it this way?" without being defensive, or self-judging, a whole new level of freedom and power is available.

The practices that I do and that I teach are based in principles of New Thought teachings and the Law of Attraction. Much has been written about the principles of spiritual law and the laws of the Universe. My friend Pam Grout (www.pamgrout.com) is the author of two books, *E-Squared* and *E-Cubed*. Each book offers nine experiments to prove your thoughts create your reality. I hope you will read Pam's books as well as many others that have you understand that you are the only one creating the reality you live in.

Even if you don't completely believe it, practicing the principles I will talk about in this book will take you out of the role of victim or martyr, and will put you in the driver's seat of your life. Who doesn't want that?

In Shawn Achor's book, *The Happiness Advantage*, he talks about how Einstein's Theory of Relativity challenges our common understanding of the fixed nature of time. He gives the example that because of the relative nature of time and motion, a person standing still would age faster than one travelling at the speed of light. Though it challenges our common sense, which would tell us that our rate of aging should be fixed, it illuminates the relative relationship of time and motion. Even those things that seem so fixed and unchangeable, according to Einstein's theory depend a lot on where the observer stands.

Achor says, "*Relativity doesn't end with mere physics. Every second of our own experience has to be measured through a relative and subjective brain. In other words, "reality" is merely our brain's relative understanding of the world based on where and how we are observing it. Most important, we can change this perspective at any moment, and by doing so change our experience of the world around us.*"

You don't have to believe as I do, that everything is energy and we are always creating our own reality with our words, thoughts, and emotions. If you make a choice to come from the **perspective** that you are creating your own reality, and view your life through that lens, then you can be someone who takes 100% responsibility for their life. And if you can be someone who can take 100% responsibility for their life, then you are never a victim of anyone or anything. And that, my friend, is power!

I like using the term response ability or being 100% able to respond to my life, to my own moods and feelings, and life as it comes.

Being proactive instead of reactive is the number one habit in Stephen Covey's book, *The 7 Habits of Highly Successful People*. Covey writes about being 100% response able for your reactions to life.

When people come to work with me as a coach, I ask them two questions before we can start. They are: Are you willing to have a powerful and happy life? Are you willing to be held 100% responsible for creating it?

The Anatomy of a Belief

This book is intended to give you tools and perspectives that allow you to wake up and get conscious that you are the one creating your experience of reality. One of the main exercises we do in my seminars and you will do in the Practical Application section of this book is based on your BS, or Belief System.

We know today that the brain has recorded everything you have ever thought or emoted about all of your life. Whether you believe it or not, those programs or neural patterns are always running in the background of your mind, even if you don't know it or are unconscious of it.

The best example I can think of to explain this is to compare it to an iPhone. If you lightly double-click on the button at the bottom of the screen, all the programs or websites you have opened in the past will pop up. You need to take your finger and swipe them away to close them. They have been running in the background using your battery life even though you didn't see them, and probably weren't aware that they were there. The same is true with your BS (Belief System). It is always running in the background whether you are aware or not, and it may be sapping your energy, or working counter to what you say you want.

A belief is just something that you have told yourself over and over and over again. Some beliefs come from our cultural and family backgrounds, and some we made up based on an experience. Though we are the ones who made it up or said it to ourselves, once we have said it or affirmed it enough, we start acting like it is the truth.

One example from my life as a young person is the belief "You don't love me just the way I am." When I hit Jr. High, my mother and sisters often tried to get me to put on make-up and carry a purse because that is what girls my age were doing. At the time this embarrassed me, and I felt very ashamed and uncomfortable. I decided that they, "don't love me just the way I am." I had evidence because they consistently asked me to do things like put on make-up, which made me uncomfortable. This continued to be my evidence that they didn't love me the way I was. With maturity, age, and common sense, I am now very clear that my sisters and my mom were just doing what culture dictated them to do. It had nothing to do with how much they loved me. Yet at the time it validated my feelings of separation and insecurity and allowed me to be the victim of their attention.

To understand this BS even more clearly, let me outline the anatomy of a belief. A belief starts with a thought. It's just a thought. However, that thought elicits an emotion. The emotion then gives validity to the thought. Since we now have emotions about this thought, it must be true. Then we start speaking the thought, which makes it even more true. After thinking, feeling, and speaking these thoughts, we start to behave like this is all true, and that solidifies our belief in stone.

Here's the example I gave earlier:

Thought: You don't love me the way I am.

Emotion: Sad, upset, embarrassed

I start speaking and thinking all this to myself and I have evidence because my sisters and mom keep trying to get me to put on make-up.

I start acting like they don't love me the way I am. I do things like be angry and surly with them. Their complaints about my behavior solidify the thought.

It has become my truth that, "you don't love me the way I am".

Here's another one that many people can relate to:

Thought: I can't get a handle on my weight loss.

Emotion: Sad, depressed, overwhelmed, resigned

Speaking: "I can't get a handle on my weight loss, I should just give up…"

Behavior: Eating every cookie in the house.

Evidence: Look, I just ate every cookie in the house, I really can't get a handle on my weight loss.

Can you see how important it is to understand that your thoughts create beliefs about yourself? Later in the book when we get to practical application, I will have you get clear about what you say about the areas of your life you would like to change or transform. Each thing you say started out as just a thought. By now they are beliefs you have about yourself, but they started as a thought and can be undone the same way.

In my experience, all people are run by their BS. The key is to start to create them on purpose, because how you believe it will go is how it will go.

Your Operating System

Another way to gain awareness is to understand that you have an operating system. You have your BS, which is all based on your past, but the other part that is affected by your past are your brain centers. I am not a neuroscientist; in fact, I know just enough to be dangerous. However, some basic understanding of the brain and how it works can really empower us.

In his work on *Emotional Intelligence*, Daniel Goleman coined the term "amygdala hijack" to describe the physiological activity of the brain and its impact on our cognitive abilities when we are faced with an event that activates our "fight or flight" response. Just having this awareness is huge. Cultivating this awareness puts us in a position of power because when we can observe the automatic system at work, we are no longer blindly reacting, but can begin to step in and choose a response in line with how we want to show up in the world.

Here is the basic understanding of hijack that I share with clients:

There is a part of your brain called the amygdala. Its job is to be a sentry or lookout for threat. It serves to keep you safe. So it sits and looks for threat. When a threat is perceived, the amygdala activates a process that releases a hormone called cortisol into your brain. This initiates your freeze, flight or fight response.

When your brain gets flooded by this hormone, your reasoning brain (left and right prefrontal cortex) gets washed out. The bridge is out. Do not enter. When this part of your brain is washed out, you get stupid and reactive. This is when you say childish regressive statements like, "always" and "never" (e.g., "you 'never' contribute around here," or, "you 'always' take his side"). This is useful if your life is in danger and you need to react rather than weigh options, but not so useful when dealing with your boss or your spouse/partner/significant other.

When hijacked, you are being run by your limbic system, not your reasoning brain. You are confused and have a hard time remembering things. Once activated, your body needs time to process the hormone or "come down" from the hijack. Otherwise, the likelihood of it happening again is high.

My advice to people is to "Shut Your Mouth." I am a mouthy person and if I am functioning under a hijack I can get myself into trouble. I have to shut my mouth and find a way to come down.

It sometimes feels like everyone around you really is just being an asshole. If it seems like everyone and everything is out to ruin your day, I promise you have been triggered or hijacked by something or someone.

The practice to build awareness is to start to notice earlier and earlier when you have been hijacked. When it happens in an argument, I suggest you shut your mouth. I suggest couples and businesses use the vernacular "hijacked" with each other so that they can know what is happening.

You are not able to be rational when you are hijacked, so please wait to respond to any correspondence – especially with people that you love – because it's when you are hijacked that you say things you cannot take back. The more you practice awareness of your own responses and triggers and once you start to really clean out your past, the faster you will be able to talk yourself down from a hijack.

Universal Truth Principles

I mentioned spiritual law before, and I hope you will make learning more about spiritual law part of your journey. My favorite book to recommend is *The Game of Life and How to Play It* by Florence Scovel Shinn. Florence will educate you on the law, of which she is very clear.

Again, I have no care about what you believe about spiritual law. And in order to give you practical tools that will serve your personal growth, I want you to be at least conscious of the principles that follow. If you don't believe them, you can still use the tools to serve you by just being conscious and flexing your muscle around your awareness.

What You Focus On Gets Bigger

Any coach, or personal development person considers this a no-brainer, but it's so important to always notice where your focus is. Are you focusing on good behavior in your children or what they don't do well? The same would be true for your lover or spouse. What you focus your thoughts and energy on will always expand. Unfortunately, as human beings we have a tendency to focus and speak about what we don't want rather than what we do want. We go around saying things like "I'm broke", "I can never get ahead in my finances", "weight loss is an uphill battle", "I can't get a handle on my weight". In both cases, you are focusing on and giving energy to what you don't want - the weight and the debt. As long as that is your focus, your results will be unfavorable. Instead, you want to focus on what you want. Focus on building wealth and getting healthy. What you focus on gets bigger.

What you focus on gets bigger. That's all there is to it. It's common sense. Everybody knows it if you really think about it and pay attention to what you're focusing on in your life. When you are expecting or wanting a child, you notice children and babies everywhere. When you purchase or want a particular kind of car, you start noticing them frequently.

What I want for you is to become masters at looking at the results that you're producing in your life and asking, "Where the heck is my focus?" If I am having a bunch of negativity show up in my life, if I'm having a bunch of failure, if I'm having a bunch of drama, where is my focus if that's what's there? You want to become masters at looking at what you are already producing, the results you're already producing and asking yourself, "Where is my focus?"

Letting Go Of Attachment

Joe Vitale, author and law of attraction teacher, says, "You can have anything you want in your life as long as you don't need it". This is a common concept in personal development and spiritual circles. It takes practice to notice when you are focused on something so much that you are "attached" to it. Attachment energetically causes resistance, resistance to anything that does not perfectly match your ideal vision. I think of it as being like a dog with a bone. That dog will not play catch, chase cars, let people pet it, or interact in a friendly way with other dogs when it is focused on that bone. When your gums are bleeding and your friends are annoyed, you need to let it go.

Noticing attachment is a practice of awareness. There is a difference in the energy of working toward a goal and exhausting mental and physical energy obsessing about it. I can feel in my body when I hold that kind of energy. I notice, or at times have had friends tease me, when I constantly talk about something. When I get focused on that thing and I can't let it go, it becomes an exercise of the ego. I'm going to do what I want and I'm going to have it my way. The more I get like that, the less it's going to manifest, and the less capable I become of seeing better options or ways to achieve my ultimate goal.

As humans we all do this at some level. It's a universal principle that when we are attached to an outcome or too attached to how things look we can keep them from being created. We see examples of this in daily life, but we just don't name it and use it consciously. Many of us know couples who tried desperately to have a child, and the minute they adopted a child, she gets pregnant. You may have known someone desperately seeking true love, yet they consistently hit brick walls. The minute they give up and stop trying so hard, they meet someone and fall in love – or notice someone who had been there all along.

In both of these cases, they let it go and it manifested. She finally gave up searching for the right guy, the right guy shows up in her back yard. In our practical world we would say, "Oh, they gave up". The reality is they allowed it to happen. They let go. They stopped resisting.

What You Resist Persists

I heard myself say many times that I would never write a book. I also said I would never actually go on testosterone and transition, I would never move back to Kansas… It seems as though all things in my life that I swear "I will never…" I actually end up doing, and doing big. I now understand that this is a universal law. Simply, what you resist persists. Having a clear understanding of this and seeing it as a universal truth is one of the tools I use and teach my clients to use to live an easier life.

The pattern of resistance persisting is easy to spot in others. You may know someone who, as my friend Annola Charity puts it, is always dating "the same guy, just in different pants." You or a friend may consistently have an overbearing or unreasonable boss regardless of how many times you've changed jobs. Pema

Chodron, a Buddhist nun, says, *"nothing ever goes away until it has taught us what we need to know… it just keeps returning with new names, forms, manifestations until it has taught us what we need to know"*. When we can stop defending our position or running away from the overbearing boss or bad boyfriend, we can be open to what there is to learn from our resistance.

It's a simple process to notice when you are resisting something or have resistance around a topic. It takes practice, but once you get good at understanding what it looks like and feels like when you are resisting something, you can identify your focus and go to work shifting it from what you don't want to what you do want. It is common sense that when someone speaks a truth you don't want to face you become defensive. That is resistance. Our goal is to start to identify when you are resisting.

Resistance is a road map, or built-in signal system to help you get to the heart of the matter, or source of your suffering. Though it occurs as if you are angry about what just happened with your boss or significant other, resistance illuminates an underlying belief or thought pattern that was put in place long before the current incident. If you have an unconscious belief that you don't deserve to be happy, or that no one really cares about you, you will continually experience that in the words and actions of your significant other until you heal or shift that belief for yourself.

It will be a muscle you start to flex. The practice is becoming conscious/aware of your resistance by recognizing what it feels like. You've got to start to know for yourself what does resistance look like for you? For me it shows up as anger, discomfort, being right about something, thinking that people should do what I say they should do.

What you resist persists. It will keep coming at you stronger. You've got to find a way to look at the results in your life and ask, "What am I resisting?" If I've got someone continuing to come at me with a particular issue, I'm probably resisting that person or resisting that issue. Especially if something keeps coming at you the same way over and over.

What you focus on gets bigger, letting go of attachment, what you resist persists, these are the three spiritual or universal principles I want you to notice. Now that you know, you can start building your own awareness of them functioning in your own life. You can start to practice noticing when you are attached, resisting, and where your focus is.

It's a practice and you will never master it completely but you can get really good at being able to choose to release and let go rather than try to control. The more you do it, the easier it gets.

Recommended reading for conscious creating and spiritual law, as well as building awareness:

Ask and It Is Given by Esther and Jerry Hicks
The Attractor Factor by Joe Vitale
The Awakening Course by Joe Vitale
E-Squared by Pam Grout
E-Cubed by Pam Grout
The Game of Life and How to Play It by Florence Scovel Shinn

CHAPTER 3

Introducing SELF and SMALL

We have all heard many times that to be successful you must "believe in yourself". We are familiar with quotes like, "To thine own self be true," and "Know thyself". Let's take a look at defining and deepening our understanding of "self".

I view SELF as the part of you that is connected to all that is. Call it God, Higher Self, or the Universe, your SELF is the piece of you that is eternal. It's your intuition. The smart part of you. The part of you that advises against that next drink or piece of pie or hurtful retort. The part of you that wants only to be loving and kind and to take the high road no matter what. It's the part of you that knows you are loved.

I know a lot of people don't distinguish between religion and spirituality, or have some hurt or disgust around religion. My goal is a deepened self-awareness, not religious conversion, so to be accessible to everyone I came up with an acronym for the SELF.

SELF = Spiritually Evolved Loving Friend

Leaning inside is about connecting with your own SELF. I know from my own experience and from coaching for thousands of hours that when you focus on feeding your SELF it will serve you beyond your understanding. You will be able to stretch time, calm fears and get into a flow of life that is magnificent and easy.

The game is to always have your eye on whether you are empowering your SELF or your SMALL.

For example, one thing you can start to practice immediately is to ask your SELF, "How can I see this from a spiritually evolved place." You can ask your SELF for guidance. It will never let you down. You just have to practice listening to it and start to understand what it means to feed it. My seven steps are designed to feed and to honor the SELF. They are about putting the oxygen mask on your SELF first.

SMALL

One of the goals of becoming a conscious person is to start to observe and watch your SMALL. How many times have we heard, "Don't play small" or "Playing small doesn't serve you?" What does it really mean to play small?

What I call SMALL, some would call the ego acting out or misbehaving, and I could make an argument for the two being interchangeable. If that term helps you in your awareness, by all means use it. For the purposes of distinguishing and accessing our power to transform our experience of life I am introducing you to your SMALL.

The SMALL is all the ways that you behave, including your thoughts, actions, and attitudes, when you are NOT being your highest, best SELF. All the ways you behave that are the **opposite** of being loving and connected.

What I want for you is to get to the point where you can observe and laugh at yourself when you catch yourself playing small. Laugh at yourself because you are a human being and all of us play small. All of us, depending on our mood, how much sleep we've had, how much sugar we have consumed, how stressed we are, can be reactive and cranky.

In his book, *Polishing the Mirror: How to Live from your Spiritual Heart*, Ram Dass identifies this power of self-observation as the "witness".

> *"The witness doesn't evaluate; it doesn't judge your actions. It merely makes note of them. It's a subtle thing, the watcher watching him or herself watching. It's actually two planes of consciousness simultaneously, the witness and the ego. The witness is connected to the soul plane."*

I find as a coach that women, in particular, when they observe their SMALL can get caught up in shame and guilt. This kind of thinking separates us from connection to SELF. Shifting to interest or amusement toward your automatic thought processes is the goal. Thoughts happen automatically, but you can observe and choose your focus.

It is powerful for you to know your default ways of being when faced with stress so that you can begin to intervene, and make choices around how you want to behave. Becoming conscious of how you "be" is what gives you the power to choose and start to really create your life from a place of power.

I want for you to be able to love yourself enough to not even judge yourself when you play small. But instead, forgive yourself immediately and make a choice about how you will be in the moment.

In order to bring a bit of levity as well as consciousness to your behavior, I invite you to create an acronym for your SMALL.

You can create your own, or borrow from some that the people in my seminars created. Here are a few examples:

S - Superficial, Silent, Sarcastic, Snarky, Self-absorbed, Stressed, Stubborn, Secluded, Shallow, Scared, Smart Ass, Silly, Stand Offish, Snappy, Scarce, Scarcity Minded

M - Mouthy, Mad, Manipulative, Mean, Manic, Moody, Melodramatic, Morose, Melancholy, Mediocre, Minimizing, Me-focused, Martyr

A - Asshole, Ass (Pain in the), Angry, Avoiding, Absent, Attached, Alienated, Aloof, Arrogant, Acidic, Anxious, Agreeable

L - Loud, Lazy, Lethargic, Late, Low

L - Lippy, Loser, Lewd, Lacking, Lame, Living
in the Past

By naming and claiming your SMALL you can start to bring awareness to your own behavior and ways of being that are not what you want for your life. Awareness is the goal here. Waking up to how you are really living and starting to take steps toward a life that you consciously create.

Most people are still completely unconscious to the way we create our own reality through our thoughts, observations, and beliefs. That leaves them reacting by default to outside circumstance. I am clear that we create our experience of reality. The more conscious/aware you become of your SMALL and your SELF, the more choice you have. The more choice you have the more power you have.

LEAN INSIDE

7 Steps to Personal Power

Down and Dirty Version:

Sorry you've had to wait until this point in the book just to get to the actual seven steps. Without further ado, these are the steps:

1. Commit
2. Get happy
3. Get clear about what you want, and ask
4. Baby step it out:
   a. Speaking
   b. Action
5. Accountability: Put in accountability structures like crazy
6. Imagine it
7. Turn it over

Repeat, Repeat, Repeat…

Step 1: Get On the Path – Commit – Close the Back Door

Commit to a path of transformation. By that I mean continually chipping away at everything that is NOT your highest, best SELF by practicing progress not perfection. Commit to being on a continual path of growth and transformation throughout your life. Transformation is continual progression, not perfection. Know that your focus has everything to do with your experience of life. This also means being committed to never getting it done, and being willing to get 100% responsible for creating it.

My intention for this book is that it be a starting point. I am thrilled when sharing my insights and experience has someone begin a path of transformation. There is no end, but a beginning is necessary. This is a practical guide to transformation. In order to create results, you have to commit to the practice part of the practicality.

In my seminars I have women write themselves a letter from their SELF. A letter with a date in your journal serves a declaration that you can go back to over and over again to remind you that you have already committed, and there is no turning back. It serves as a line of demarcation that you have begun your journey. There still may be days when you choose to pull the covers over your head. Remember it's about progress not perfection. Declare that you are on that path of uncovering your highest, best SELF for the rest of your life, and even if you take a day off or wander down a side road, you will remain on that path.

I invite you to consider the following to be included as the things you will commit to on this path of personal growth and transformation:

1. No quitting - I agree to never, never, never, never quit on creating happiness and fulfillment in my life. I know I can transform anything that gets in my way. I know I can count on myself to keep making progress and therefore I also commit to practicing constant forgiveness for myself and others.
2. No making yourself wrong - I am not allowed to cuss myself, call me names, and threaten myself. I will cease negative self-talk, and commit to talking to myself like I would a good friend.
3. Give up or close the door on being a victim or martyr.
4. Commit to getting to know my SELF: I agree to keep giving up that I am anything but a full expression of Love, therefore I can count on my SELF to keep dismantling stories that keep me small and fearful.

As I mentioned before, I do all this work myself and coach others to create their own path of transformation. What there is to know is that it takes practice. I am a personal and spiritual development practitioner. Basically this means that I practice. I practice, and I practice, and I practice. I have to keep at it because some of the old programs that run in my head are angry and destructive. Now that you know my past, it isn't a stretch to figure out that some of my patterns of behavior may not be the most productive.

Many people believe that transformation happens in an instant. When a person is doing personal development work, they will have insights, or will be able to see something or learn something about themselves that they haven't seen before. That insight or blind spot revealed can change a person in that instant. Those "aha" moments shift our perceptions of ourselves and reality and open up new futures. However, my experience with both myself and all the people I have coached is that those insights, "aha" moments, and blind spots revealed will go right back to their old hiding places if action is not taken and practice is not ongoing. I have come to the understanding that transformation is chipping away at everything that is not your highest, best SELF by practicing progress not perfection. It may appear that a caterpillar transforms into a butterfly in an instant as it emerges from its cocoon without effort. In reality there is a ton of work happening in that cocoon. Sometimes becoming the best SELF you can be feels like one step forward and two steps back.

One tool on the path of progress not perfection is to create a practice of constant forgiveness. I find that almost all women have some level of perfectionism that runs them. It keeps them from starting things because they can't see how to do it perfectly, or beating themselves up over whatever didn't meet their ideal. I remember vividly the day that I realized I was being run by perfectionism and the impact it had on my life.

It was a day like any other day. It was my job to drop the kids off at day care before my work day began. It started off as a good morning. I got up, got both kids fed and dressed, and in the car without incident. As I was backing the car out of the driveway, I realized that I hadn't made coffee. Part of my morning routine for all of my marriage is to be the one to make coffee for my beloved. In the instant that I remembered I didn't make coffee, I got unusually angry with myself. I was so frustrated that I hadn't checked off everything. I missed the coffee. After I dropped off the kids I was coaching myself through the incident and anger. Rationally, I knew that my level of upset didn't really make sense. My wife wasn't even upset that there wasn't coffee, yet here I was, emotionally responding as though something horrible had happened. It was then that I asked myself, "Jay, what if you never get each box checked off? What if you never get it right? Can you still love yourself?"

If you operate at a high level of perfectionism, you may have a strong response to that last statement. Can you still love yourself even if you never get it all right? In that moment I wanted to throw up. I thought, "Hell NO! I will get it right. I will get to the point where I check every box." Wow! I observed myself having such a strong reaction. Even the thought of giving up having to do it right made me freak out. It was very telling for me. It was then in the observation that I realized I was being run by perfectionism. I could clearly see the cost on me (stress), my kids (angry, weird dad), and Jessica (stressed out, angry, weird husband). In that moment, I realized that I had to forgive myself for missing the coffee. I realized then in order for me to be a happy and powerful person, that constant, minute-by-minute forgiveness of myself and others was an absolute must in my life.

This story illustrates me observing and acting out my SMALL responses (snippy, mad, angry, lacking, living in the past) and choosing instead a response from my Spiritually Evolved Loving Friend.

It is often the case when I finally figure something out on my own that I am led to read other resources that confirm my own findings. Naturally, since what we focus on gets bigger. About two months after I had this epiphany, and had shared with my coach and my power posse, that constant forgiveness was something I realized all of us had to practice, I was introduced to the book *The Four Spiritual Laws of Prosperity* by Edwene Gaines. In Edwene's book she talks about practicing constant forgiveness as one of the four spiritual laws of prosperity. I was grateful to be validated in this way.

I promise that if you start practicing constant forgiveness, and you don't quit, and you keep being willing to seek your highest, best SELF, you can and will create anything in your life that you want. You have to stay on the path. You will have teachers come and go and you will learn from the most unlikely of events and people. If you don't quit, you can and you will transform your life.

Here is your first assignment:

Get a blank book or journal or notebook. Write your little pitiful sad self or SMALL a letter from your SELF. Write from the part of you that knows you can do it, the part of you that is intuitive, kind, compassionate, and resilient.

In this letter you are to make a declaration. A declaration that as of this date, you are on a path to transform your life and clear out anything that is in the way of your true happiness. My request is that you get really bold and declare your willingness to give up being a victim or martyr. You can give up self-pity and playing small. Declare yourself as a powerful person who makes a difference in the world.

Once you write this letter, you will have taken your first step on the path of transformation, and now you can never go back. From this day forward, you commit to progress not perfection, to knowing your SELF. You will have breakdowns. You will have days when you say "Forget it! I just want to wallow in my own self-pity, eat bonbons, and watch trashy TV." That is OK. You can always go back to your letter to remind yourself of your own commitment to your happiness and to knowing your true SELF.

OK, go get that journal and write the letter. I invite you to share it with a few people you really trust, or post it to my website or your own. Go get busy.

Step 2: Get to a Happy Place by Owning All Of It

You are creating your life through your own perception of the world. Though it most often occurs that we see and interpret the world as it is, it would be more accurate to say we see and experience the world as we are.

This is a concept taught by personal development practitioners and experts like myself. It is supported by the studies of physics, psychology, spirituality, and neuroscience. As I've said, this is not new information, nor am I an expert in every one of the above fields; however, I know through my own experience, studies, and the experiences of my clients that it is a game changing realization.

The bottom line is that if you are an unhappy, sad, or angry person, the reality that you create is unhappy, sad, and angry.

After making the commitment to be willing and never give up, the most important piece of this formula is to get to a happy place. Finding a way to access gratitude and happiness is an absolute must.

This is where the practice comes in. You must practice gratitude. You have to find a way to feel grateful for what you currently have no matter what.

When a person is still struggling with the base level of Maslow's five basic needs (from his *Hierarchy of Needs*), those basic survival needs must be addressed first. Do you have enough food? Do you have clothing and shelter? If you do, then you can start being grateful for that. The reality is that many people, even in the wealthiest countries in the world, do not have reliable access to food, clothing, and shelter. Being able to meet those needs is something for which many of us can be grateful.

For the purposes of this book, I am going to assume that you are already able to meet your needs for physical survival.

Given that, my formula for getting to a happy place follows.

Know Thy Self

Ultimately, it is your job to figure out how to get yourself happy. I can make recommendations and share information, but you must identify what resonates with you.

Please Note: Listed below are things you will do for the rest of your life. You are never done. A happy, powerful life is a journey not a destination. You have to practice and keep at it. Just when you think you have it all handled, you will get to a new level. It will get easier and more automatic over time because you will get faster and faster at aligning with your SELF.

You have to clean out everything physically, emotionally, intellectually, and energetically that could be in the way of your happiness.

Get complete with your past: All of us have a past. Some of our past has been handed to us. We inherit limited thinking and fears from our parents, grandparents, and cultures. You have to take a good look at this stuff. Get your head around the fact that you are run by your past. Where you came from, how much money you had growing up, how much abuse you have experienced or dealt out impacts your perception. If you have a parent that is an alcoholic, guess what? You are an adult child of an alcoholic. Your relationship patterns are screwed up because of that. In order to really create a powerful life, you have to deal with and heal that little kid inside of you that is afraid of intimacy. You may need to get your butt to therapy. Start reading books that address things pertinent for you. Get engaged and response able for your own past and life. Read books on happiness. I recommend *The Happiness Advantage* by Shawn Achor. Read books that teach you about your brain and happiness or how your brain works. Some of my clients like Joey Klein's book, *The Inner Matrix*, or *Super Brain* by Deepak Chopra and Rudolph Tanzi. Get support and start figuring out how your brain works. Address your past, so you don't keep dragging old baggage into the present. You can work in tandem with a therapist and a good coach. The bottom line is, you have to stop pretending that you are fine when you are F.I.N.E. (Fucked up, Insecure, Neurotic and Emotional). Develop your Emotional Intelligence and your Spiritual Intelligence. Deal with your stuff and take 100% responsibility for it. Stop blaming your parents or anyone else for your failed relationships or unhappiness. Get willing to deal with your stuff and get your past complete. Engage in transformational programs, books and get in action. Just get willing and start cleaning out any and all excuses that have to do with your childhood or your past.

Reframe/Re-tell your disempowering stories: Now that you have started to deal with your past, start learning to tell a new story. If you had asked me to tell you my story when I was 19 years old, I would have told you a sob story about my alcoholic father and checked out mother. In my story I was the victim and at that young age, I got a lot of juice out of my tale of tragic woe. Today, I would honestly describe my dad as a pillar of his community, as he was the mayor of our small town, and my mom as a saint. She had 9 children and I knew she was really mad when she used the phrase, "listen here, lamb chop." I can only tell that story now because I have taken 100% responsibility and healed up my past. I know that my parents did the best job they could. Raising nine kids on very little income was tough. They didn't have the skills to help me deal with being a queer kid and I hid that from them. That was my response to my life. Now I am able to respond more powerfully to my world. I take full responsibility for creating it.

Start telling a new story that has you show up in the world as powerful, not as a victim or martyr in any way. We are inspired by stories of those who overcome obstacles and thrive despite their circumstances. Start by retelling and reframing those stories in which you cast yourself as the victim.

Retrain your brain: Your brain has been programmed by your past experience. For the most part, you weren't aware the programming was taking place and it now runs on autopilot.

Research shows that we are only conscious of a small amount of what is going on in our minds. This book and all my work is designed to have you become more conscious. Wake up!

Your brain has neural patterns that were formed very early on in your life. Most of the time you are not actually acting but reacting using whatever response patterns are ingrained in your system as effective ways to survive, avoid pain or embarrassment, or keep yourself safe. Your brain just runs those reactions to stimuli like it breathes for you and beats your heart - without your conscious awareness. It is a computer, and, if you ask me, it has a glitch. The glitch is that we all have patterns that just run all the time in response to whatever stimuli are before us. Even when those responses are inappropriate and make no sense when you actually examine them.

It takes focus on healing and retraining to stop old patterns and create new ones. One of the most powerful tools being recognized in our world today to retrain the brain is meditation. You can find all kinds of research on meditation and the brain with a quick internet search. Do that. Go learn about your brain. Learn how it works and decide for yourself if it is serving you or limiting you. Do your own investigation of your brain and consider practicing meditation, and any other brain technique you can find, that will serve you to replace old patterns of behavior and thinking that limit you from being your most powerful SELF.

Some books I recommend on this are *Super Brain* by Deepak Chopra and Rudolph Tanzi, *Budda's Brain* by Dr. Rick Hanson, and *How the Mind Works* by Steven Pinker. Read the literature or watch TED talks on neuroscience for ways to understand how your brain and your operating system works.

Forgiveness: Practice constant forgiveness. There may be some forgiveness that needs to happen as you complete your past, so that you can own your own power and release old hurts. I know we covered that already, but I can't iterate enough that forgiveness has to be a constant, minute to minute practice. Especially in the beginning when you become aware of your automatic operating system, and start noticing what a total ass you are. You have to forgive yourself a million times a day, sometimes in addition to forgiving others. A constant practice of forgiveness is another way to practice being conscious and aware of your behavior. If you give up judging yourself for misbehavior and instead own and forgive your behaviors, it allows you the room to choose something different. Constantly berating yourself for acting out and or being less than loving, only continues to perpetuate the cycle. It's like it gives you the opportunity to be "right" about how rotten you are. That shame spiral will only reinforce your disempowering behaviors and get you nowhere fast. Forgiveness is key.

Happiness and productivity workout: Below you will find my "Happiness and Productivity Workout." I use this tool in my seminars and workshops. I invite you to read through and score yourself. The point is to have you focus on and start creating practices that will increase your consciousness and create space that will lead to your happiness and productivity.

A life of happiness and productivity is a daily commitment that takes practice. Like working out in a gym, it takes consistent action to achieve the desired result. When you first start a workout program, you find that you have sore muscles in places you didn't know you had muscles. The commitment to create happiness is the same. Your sore positive muscles show up as extra chatter in your brain, second-guessing yourself, and sometimes even emotional stress such as anger, confusion, or sadness. These are all normal sore muscles. When you make a commitment to create a positive focus, it takes time and practice to be good at it. These are muscles to flex and you will likely find some to be easier to put into practice than others. Remember that this journey is about progress not perfection. The most important thing is to do the work. Reading about squats will not tighten your glutes. Trying them one time and quitting because they seem hard won't either. The same is true for these practices. Just like the gym, some of us have further to go than others, but your happiness is worth it, and if you stick to it, you will see positive results.

Happiness and Productivity Work Out

For quickest results, I suggest focusing on the area you find most challenging. Rate yourself on a scale of 1 to 10. Some of these may already be strengths for you and some you might find challenging. Revisit weekly to observe how you shift in these areas.

1. **Prioritize time for yourself**: Do whatever rejuvenates you, makes you feel good – and good about yourself. Sports, yoga, time with friends, reading for pleasure, being in nature, music, art. Putting the oxygen mask on your SELF first gives you energy and vitality for whatever you are up to. *"The opposite of play isn't work, it's depression"* - Brian Sutton-Smith. Too often, though, doing things for pleasure rather than results gets treated like a luxury a busy person just can't afford. Flex your muscle by adding a weekly or better yet, daily "just for fun" item to your calendar.

2. **Watch your mouth**: Notice how you speak about your life. Speak only those words that match the vision you have for yourself and your life. Only speak to yourself the way you would a good friend. Positive self-talk is a practice to master. Give up gossip. Before you say something to others ask, "Is it kind, is it necessary, is it true?". Give up complaining. If you have a complaint, you have a request. Identify the underlying request, and then make that request of the right person. Make

requests from a respectful, positive place with a commitment to make a difference and to not stir up drama or trouble.

3. **Cultivate gratitude**: Find a way to practice gratitude every day. Wake up with a "thank you" on your lips. Flexing your muscle in this area could mean keeping a gratitude journal, saying out loud, "I am grateful for _____", gratitude sharing at mealtime. When you find yourself going down a rabbit hole of worry or fear, shift your thoughts to appreciation for your life. Make it a practice to be a grateful person.

4. **Create a strong personal foundation**: Do what you say you will do. Be in communication if you cannot. Care for your physical body. Get the sleep, nutrition, and exercise you need to function effectively. Get things in working order, including your house, car, and checkbook. Flexing your muscle in these areas could look like moving to a calendar system with an alarm, setting a bedtime for yourself, scheduling that overdue oil change, or organizing your sock drawer. Small bites in this area can make a huge impact on your life.

5. **Shift your perspective**: Give up taking anything personally, or assuming that people's actions are about you. Notice when you are offended by someone's words or actions. Practice asking questions and getting curious instead of paranoid. Take the opportunity to discover something about your own belief system. Shift your focus from what is not working for you to how

you can be of service. As Abraham Lincoln said, "*We can complain because rose bushes have thorns, or rejoice because thorn bushes have roses.*" Don't concern yourself with the rose bush, concern yourself with how you perceive it. Move your thoughts toward higher ground.

6. **Become aware of your operating system**: Understand your emotional and chemical brain response system. Get to know your default behavior patterns. Pay attention to the ways you may sabotage your own success and you will see patterns that lead to your limiting beliefs and conversations. When you become aware, you open the opportunity to choose something less automatic. Unaware, we react to people and situations on autopilot as we would pull a hand back from a hot stove or hop on a bike and ride - with no conscious effort or awareness of the choice we've made, or the pattern we are calling on. Get interested in what is happening and the familiar pattern of thoughts that run when you get hijacked, defensive, fearful, and angry. Flex your muscle by asking what you can learn about yourself when tempted to blame a person or circumstance for your discomfort.

7. **Practice leaning inside and quieting your mind**: Create a practice of sitting in the silence. First just practice being the observer of your thoughts but don't stop them. Practice letting them drift past. Focus on the space in between the thoughts. Meditation is extremely effective at reducing stress. In addition to experiencing less stress, you reduce health risks. Do whatever you

do (nature, prayer, community, art) to keep yourself connected to that still small voice inside that is your true SELF.

There is nothing more important than you getting yourself to a happy place. I am clear that my job is to just be happy. I know that part of what makes us happy and fulfilled is to be of service to others. I promise you if you focus on your own happiness, especially if you find happiness through serving others, your life will start to take off in a powerful way. Knowing we make a difference is a source of true joy.

My theory is that every human being has a happiness formula. Things they can learn to keep in check so they stay at a level of happiness that has them creating their lives from a powerful and positive place. I would assert that exercise and meditation are two things that benefit every human as part of a happiness formula. I think you can be happy without doing those things. However, their impact on the human condition is worth at least investigating and knowing about.

It's your job to figure out what things make you happy and able to function at your highest best level. It's your job to figure out what works for you and to take action to create it for yourself.

Here's my formula: To be at the top of my game I must exercise, meditate, listen to music that lifts me up, limit sugar intake, do work that serves and makes a difference for others, hang with my wife a lot, spend time with friends, have social activity, and be in communication with people who practice and keep seeking spiritual principles.

When I am in check with all of the things above, I am unstoppable, courageous, loving, kind, and joyously happy. I manage setbacks with ease and experience life as a miracle. When I decide to wallow in cake and quit going to the gym, life often occurs as more challenging and I am more likely to be short-tempered and frustrated.

As my brother always said, *"Maintenance is the key"*. You are going to be working on Step 2 the rest of your life. It's an ongoing process. The minute you think you are done you are going to remember something, do something, or experience something that will need to be addressed. That ex-lover you told to screw off - you are going to have to forgive yourself and/ or forgive them. You'll always remember something else. It is always, always, always ongoing. You get the gist. Let's move on to Step 3.

Step 3: Get Clear About What You Want: Get Specific – and Ask

Okay, we are on to Step 3. Step 3 is getting clear about what you want. You've made a commitment to transformation. You are becoming a happy person. You will continue clearing out your past, reframing stories, and getting your integrity in order. Now let's turn our focus onto what you want to use your power to create.

I am constantly amazed at the number of people and clients I encounter that say they don't know what they want. Being a parent of young children, I can see that my kids are very clear about what they want. Did life train us to become people that don't know? Certainly we knew when we were little. Yet person after person I encounter tells me they don't know what they want.

Of course, this doesn't apply to all women or all people. Some of you are good at this. Some of you can easily identify what you want. For those of you who are clear about what you want and are not afraid to say what you want, I ask you to be more specific. Get as specific as you can. Put in deadlines and dates. Write out any and all specifics you can imagine.

When I take a closer look it becomes more obvious that as kids, we do get our wants questioned and suppressed pretty often. I'm already doing it to my children, and I can't stop myself because we have these rules in society that say you can't pick up a cup and throw it across the restaurant just because you want to. So, I train my son to stop it and act right! I don't recommend we stop teaching manners, hygiene, and consideration for others. I recognize, though, that early training tells us all to question the validity of what we want.

I believe this is something that women, especially, learn growing up. Women are taught and expected to take care of everyone else first, and put their own desires last. Eventually that manifests as being someone without an opinion, or clarity about what they want, or someone who feels guilty about wanting anything. Part of this work is to practice knowing and becoming someone who knows what she wants. In one of the books I first recommend to clients, *The Success Principles*, Jack Canfield recommends flexing your muscle around becoming someone who knows what you want. Some of us need to retrain ourselves to know what we want. Some of us need to figure out what inspires us. If you are in that place where you aren't quite sure what you want or don't know what you want, I have two requests for you:

1. Give up saying that you don't know what you want. You've got to get how powerful your words are. When you are speaking that you "don't know what you want" you reinforce the truth of the statement and leave no room for what you want to come forth. I know it occurs like you are just stating a fact, but I know from my own experience the power of shifting one's perspective and speaking in this area.

2. Get committed to figuring out what you want. Choose something to say to support that commitment when the words, "I don't know what I want" appear on the tip of your tongue. "I am figuring out what I want". "I am on a journey of self-discovery". "I am uncovering my true passion". Use whatever words connect you to your commitment.

Those two things create massive results for my clients in this area, and did for me. This is how it happened for me: I was walking along with one of the most powerful coaches I've ever been with in my life. She is someone who listened to me so powerfully that I couldn't get away with ever playing small. I was complaining about my job. At that point I was married to the love of my life, living in a place I loved, making good money, and doing all kinds of fun stuff. For the most part I loved my life. I even loved the company where I worked, and my coworkers. I just wasn't interested in the actual work I was doing. I was working as the Director of Project Management for a furniture dealership. I was also in charge of wood home office furniture. I spent a lot of my day dealing with problems like someone having their wood desk arrive in the wrong finish, or scratched or damaged in some way. I had grown tired of this job and felt unfulfilled in my work.

So here I was complaining about it, and she said to me, "Jay Pryor, for who you are for the world, you need to either shut up about that or do something about it." I immediately retorted, "Well, if I knew what I wanted to do, I'd do it." She said, "You need to give that up." Incredulously, I replied, "Give that up? You mean **give up that I don't know what I want to do?**" As soon as the words left my mouth, it was like a lightbulb went on over my head. I could see that by continuing to say and believe "I don't know what I want," it was keeping me in the same old loop over and over again. It occurred to me that I'd been so committed to saying that I didn't know what I wanted that that was the only thing that could show up. I said, "Fine. I'll give up that I don't know what I want to do, and, in fact, I'll take on that I do know what I want to do and I just haven't told myself yet." Even though I was still being a bit of a smart ass with that retort, I did make a commitment to stop saying, "I don't know what I want."

It was eye opening to realize that saying, "I don't know what I want," had become a habit. I would catch myself mid-sentence saying it. When I did I would stop, and instead say, "What I want is on its way, and I am committed to discovering my passion."

Within a week I was noticing that I did know what I wanted my life to look like. I knew I wanted to work for myself, and I wanted to be able to do my job from anywhere. Most important, I was clear that I wanted to make a difference for other people in my work.

About a month or so later, I was coaching a leadership program. The six people I was coaching had certain measures that they were supposed to meet for the program. All six of them were failing miserably at meeting those measures. However, they were thriving in every other area of their lives. Their relationships were on fire. They were getting new jobs. They were getting their health and well-being together and just thriving in every area of life except the program where they were supposed to be meeting these measures. Someone came up to me and said, "Jay, you make a much better life coach than you do a coach for this program." I'd never heard of the term "life coach." I was like, "What did you say? Life coach? What's a life coach? You mean there's such a thing as a life coach?"

I knew immediately that this was what I was supposed to do. I went home and researched what a life coach was and how to become one. I discovered that this profession was everything on my list. I could work for myself, do my job from anywhere, and make a difference with people.

It seemed like a miracle to me. Within a short time of giving up saying the words, "I don't know what I want," I had actually discovered exactly what I wanted, and now it was up to me to create it. It was like a bolt of lightning hit me. Had I continued to insist that "I don't know what I want" was the truth, that would have never happened. I had to stop saying it.

As I mentioned earlier, I find that women, especially, are trained to anticipate what others want, and put their wants on the back burner. This manifests itself in always feeling shafted or getting the short end of the stick. Part of waking up for women is to acknowledge that you contribute to and accept the role of anticipating what others want. We have to acknowledge that cycle and own how we contribute to it.

Here's an example: The longer I walk through the world as a man, the more I get used to NOT being expected to help in the kitchen. In my family, if I brought home a girl, my sisters would expect her to help in the kitchen and/or at least to ask, "What can I do to help?" I was trained in that conversation and way of thinking. When I was a woman, or looked like one, I was expected to help in the kitchen. One of my sisters even teased that I had a sex change to get out of doing the dishes. You may laugh, but I am here to tell you that since I look like a man now, women rarely expect me to help with those tasks. I used to be the first to ask, "How can I help?" but the longer I get treated like I am not expected to help, the less I have the thought that I "should" help.

The role I am handed is one of service as a woman. That is very clear to me now that I am viewed as a man. The goal here is to become conscious of whether your service is coming from a true desire to serve, or from a pattern that you have been trained in your entire life. The training is life sucking. The service from a place of really wanting to serve is life breathing.

My friend, author Erin Brown, pointed out to me that my own use of the image of putting the oxygen mask on yourself first to allow you to serve from a place of being filled up relied heavily on that very gender-based assumption and training. I'm grateful that she pointed out that we would NEVER say that about a man. I was not even conscious of the cultural conversation I was participating in with my focus on that image. She was so right. We would never say, "Dad's going to go play a round or two of golf so he can serve from a place of love." Puke. I take it back. Serving from love is great, but put the oxygen mask on so you can breathe easily. Do things you want to make you happy, not so you can be a better servant.

I think all people can have trouble getting clear about they want. Certainly media and society provide a lot of push for what we should want or what should make us happy. Women, I know, are often culturally handed a role that says, what you want is not important. What is important is what everyone else wants. Being of service and being conscientious of the needs of others can be fulfilling. When it is unconsciously fulfilling an outside expectation rather than a choice though, it can be a source of serious regret, resentment, and numbing out of what our souls want.

If you struggle in this area, I invite you to start with baby steps. Just check in with yourself by asking questions like "what do I want for dinner?" Check in with your gut. Make a decision. Be willing to say what you want. If you start practicing you start to know and understand what it feels like to know what you want. The more familiar you are, the faster you can recognize and discern what you want. Again, if you are already good at knowing what you want, get more specific. If not, become someone who knows what you want. The first step is giving up that you don't know.

Ask!

You have to ask for what you want. We get what we ask for all the time, but we are often unaware that we are asking. The key is to be conscious of what you are speaking and the emotional energy behind it. Take on the perspective that every word you utter is a prayer. If you walk around saying, "I wish I didn't have to go to work," don't be surprised when your job dissolves. You asked for it. When you create with intention you ask for what you want. I recommend adding the phrase "for the highest good of all concerned" to your request. This ensures that you are creating from a place of positive and good intention. Just like you can't expect your spouse to know what you want, you can't expect the Universe to know either. If you ask, it is given. I am clear about this. I think there is something energetic in the asking that puts your request in motion.

Next we take action to gain more clarity and to start the creation process. That takes us to Step 4: Baby Step it Out.

Step 4: Baby Step It Out

There are two areas where we are going to create baby steps to your goal. The first baby steps involve your speaking. We will create what I call bridge affirmations that will take you from your current speaking and beliefs in the area to a new narrative around your goal. The second will be taking baby step actions.

When we experience powerlessness and dissatisfaction in an area of life, the default mode involves speaking all about how it isn't working. Like my example above, the more you affirm that something isn't working the more it won't. What we have to do is become conscious of our language and create a new conversation or build affirmations that affirm what we do want.

Affirmations have been considered corny and have had a bad rap since back in the day when Saturday Night Live created the character Stuart Smalley and his affirmations of, "I'm good enough, I'm smart enough, and gosh darn it, people like me." In the 1980s, when the world of self-help was blowing up, and affirmations became really popular, SNL cashed in and had a blast making fun of it. The teasing created a wave of people who wrote off affirmations as silly positive thinking that didn't make a difference.

The reality is that affirmations do work, but they only work if you believe them. Think back to the anatomy of a belief. If you speak things you don't believe this will not elicit the emotion that convinces you that they are true. In other words, if you are someone who really hates yourself and experiences the emotions of hatred toward yourself and then you start to say, "I love myself", your BS (Belief System) will kick in and immediately discount the words as false. That affirmation is received by your thoughts and emotions as a lie, which will reinforce the thoughts and feelings of unworthiness.

This is why we take baby steps. We start with a baby step affirmation that you can and do believe. We usually start with words like, "I am open to...", "I am willing to...", or "I am starting to believe...".

In the Unity movement denials are used in conjunction with affirmations. I teach one denial: "I give that thought no power". This denial helps us separate our SELF from the thoughts our mind is thinking that is not in line with what we are creating. It interrupts the emotion and belief that can follow our disempowering thoughts. You are not in denial about the thought; you are denying the thought power. Byron Katie's book, *Loving What Is*, is a great resource for helping separate our thoughts from our feelings and beliefs.

Once we combine these baby step bridge affirmations with baby step actions, the actions validate the speaking and thinking. In my workshops I have women put something in their calendar as the first baby step. What is most key is that you stop the speaking and actions that affirm what you don't want. That is where the work is. Those are habits to break. Having a specific affirmation helps you redirect yourself when you fall into habitual thoughts or speaking in an area you are committed to transforming.

Every baby step helps us to further define our vision. More than a few times I have had clients come to me with a vague idea about what they want but the picture isn't clear, or is obscured by current limiting beliefs. I am blessed with a gift of sight for other people. It's part of what makes me a good coach. Often I can see a future for people that they can't see. Part of my job then is to hold the vision for them until they get to the place where they can see it themselves. What there is to know is action creates clarity. Just speaking a positive bridge affirmation such as, "I am headed in the right direction" or "I am open to receive my good", and getting into action will cause clarity to come little by little.

Jack Canfield gives an example in his book, *The Success Principles*, that even though you can only see in the light of your headlights when you drive at night, you still know you'll arrive at your destination. I live in the Midwest where we travel on I-70. I know if I start in my home town of Lawrence, KS and I drive west on I-70 I will eventually get to Colorado. I may be able to only see 25 feet ahead, but I have faith that I will make it. Getting in action creates the ability to see the next 25 feet and then the next 25 feet. Action creates clarity.

Step 4 asks you to create a new conversation and new actions in the area of your life you want to change or transform. Baby steps are all that is necessary. Remember, too, that when babies take those steps, they sometimes stumble and fall. They don't then decide that walking must not be for them, they get up and keep trying until they have it mastered. The important part is to keep at it. Habits of speaking and thinking are hard to break, so find a way to be held accountable to speak the new bridge affirmations or conversation, and to take on the new baby step actions. That takes us to Step 5.

Step 5: Put in Accountability Measures Like Crazy

Part of my job as a coach is to serve as an accountability structure for my clients around what they want to create in their lives. One reason my seminars create long term success is that when women leave, they have an accountability partner to meet with and keep up the work. They are getting together in person and online to support each other around their goals. Being a part of the group in and of itself is a level of accountability.

Bottom line, if you are really committed to creating something in your life, find a way to be held accountable for it.

We let ourselves off the hook or go unconscious easily if we don't have accountability structures in place. I say to come at it from every direction possible. Create what my friend Pam Grout calls a "power posse" similar to what I've described above. Find people who inspire you, support you, and listen to you as your highest, best SELF. Hire a coach or join a support group. Register for a class so you have to show up. Schedule time in your calendar to work on your goals or take baby steps. Set alarms to remind yourself to affirm what you want. Some people put up post it reminders in their environments to keep them present to what they are creating. Making and displaying vision boards with images and words that express the goal can keep it alive. Read books or attend webinars that keep you in the conversation of transformation and growth. Surround yourself with positive reinforcement.

Warning: Don't tell Nina. I always tell my seminar participants that as they get started with baby steps, to be sure they don't go straight to Nina - Nina Negativa. You know her, that friend who is always complaining. The one who will give you the laundry list of why life sucks, nothing works, and everyone is an idiot. When looking for your power posse or accountability buddy, make sure they are people you can count on to help hold the high watch. Especially when things are new and vulnerable, only share your vision with people you can count on to build you up, not tear you down.

If you have set up accountability structures and you don't use them, or you blow them off, don't use that opportunity to beat yourself up over what you are not doing or create a story that you can't, won't, never will. SMALL would love for you to quit. We can get juice out of proving that we are "right" that we can't have what we want. It's an opportunity to revisit your commitment to the path of transformation. You can either get back on the horse or sell the horse and buy the car you really want. Sometimes you'll find that you are not truly committed to the goal - or that you now see something better. You may need to reevaluate goals. Sometimes my clients have "shoulds" dressed in goal clothing. Perhaps what there is to do is love yourself even though that goal is not going to get met or created.

Here is an example: Often women come to work with me and part of their goals involve getting back in shape or losing weight. They do all the work internally, or so they think, and they put in accountability structures. They may hire a personal trainer, get a gym membership, and buy workout clothes. They commit to me that they will get in action. This works for a little while. Just until the new wears off or they manifest a big project that gets them too busy. This is a telltale sign to me that this goal is not really what they want. They aren't really committed to it like they say.

This is when I get to ask the best question ever. If you never lose the weight and never get back in shape, can you love yourself anyway? With many women, body image goals are "should" goals. They have them because our culture has trained them since they were girls to hate their bodies. As a teen, I didn't even like having a female body, but still felt ashamed of being too fat - though when I look back at photos I can see I was never actually overweight.

My goal in this case is to ask the woman to Lean Inside and work on knowing she is loved so she can learn to love her SELF. The more energy she gives to that the more energy she has. Often, weight loss comes easily or without even trying once they have done the work to know that they are loved. Sometimes their weight stays the same, but their appreciation for and confidence in their bodies increases to the point where they no longer feel a need to focus on that goal.

The more accountability, usually the faster results produced. I believe in paying experts for accountability. Obviously it's part of my job. If you have the money, it is good investment in yourself to hire a coach or trainer to hold you accountable. Find friends, business partners or attend courses like mine to help support you. It's your job to find a way to get accountable and response able for your goals and your direction in life. You can do it.

Step 6: Visualize /Imagine It

By now in this work you have identified habitual ways of thinking and speaking that are the lens through which you view your life. This step is your opportunity to develop new ways of thinking that lead to different outcomes. Your assignment will be to set aside time to visualize what you want your life to be like. Don't just let your imagination run amok. Harness its power for good.

By consciously taking time to imagine the new feelings and behaviors, you are setting up new neural pathways and giving your brain good chemicals. The synapses fire the same way when you imagine something as they do when you actually do it.

When you get an inspiration for something, start having fun by playing make believe in your mind. Imagine the conversations you will have when this goal is accomplished. Imagine yourself doing the things you want to do, or being the person you want to be. Imagine how you'll feel when you attain your vision. It may take years to come to fruition, but if you have an inkling of what it looks like, I invite you to start imagining it. Visualize and put out to the universe - remember everything is energy.

When inspiration hits, it is often natural to imagine this way. When you think about it, everything you've accomplished in your life you visualized first. You imagined and planned marriages, children, jobs, careers, vacations, and graduations. When you are excited about something you automatically begin to imagine how it will be to be a parent or a doctor or a wife. It is what we do.

Many times we fall back on using our imaginations to worry - create scenarios in our minds of what we don't want, and neglect to spend time and energy imagining what we do want. Exercise some new and fun neural pathways rather than just running down well-worn paths of doubt, fear, and resignation.

Now, you may not be clearly imagining the end result, but you have to be able to envision the next step and the next step, even if it's baby step visualization. Maybe you can see the end result, or what you think the end result is going to look like. Either way, spend time imagining it. Many people believe that imagination is a power that human beings have. Charles Fillmore, co-founder of Unity, lists imagination among the twelve powers of human beings. Using your imagination is a creative energy.

What I know from my own work is that when I can't see or feel a vision of my goal, it won't manifest. I have learned to strengthen my muscle of seeing possibility by setting aside time to visualize and imagine my goals.

Keep in mind that imagining and visualizing your dreams and goals is not the same as fantasizing about winning the lottery -especially if you don't ever buy a lottery ticket. I want to be clear that fantasizing about things you have no intention of actually taking action around is not visioning. That is mental masturbation. Daydreaming is fun and you can do that all you want to. Just know that it is not the same as visioning and likely won't get you any closer to winning the lottery.

Visioning is about the future you want to live into. Visioning is using your imagination to support what you are up to in life in a powerful way.

Step 7: Let It Go

When I was 19 years old and getting my act together, with the help of Alcoholics Anonymous, my sponsor had me memorize a prayer that goes with the 3rd step of the program. It goes like this:

> *God, I offer myself to Thee to do with me and build with me as Thou wilt. Relieve me from the bondage of self that I may better do Thy will. Take away my difficulties so that victory over them may bear witness to those I may help of Thy power, Thy love, and Thy way of life. May I do Thy will always.*

It's a mouthful, right? Fortunately for me, I am coachable and willing. Trusting and doing what my coaches/sponsors/ mentors/teachers told me to do has blessed my life. I memorized this prayer and said it every hour on the hour. After doing this for a couple of days, I noticed that life got a little easier. After a few weeks, I noticed that life became so much easier that I felt as if I was in the flow of something, and that I could relax and trust that I would stay afloat.

This was my first experience of truly letting go and turning my life and my will over to a higher power. The practice is meant to restore the alcoholic to sanity. We could all use some sanity restoration since we have human operating systems that can throw us into a rage over something that happened 30 years ago or something that we fear might happen. Don't you think? When we allow the automatic pattern of thoughts and responses to everything from the frustration of traffic to the loss of a business account be our final truth, we drive ourselves nuts. Our BS blocks our own clarity of vision and peace of mind when we see it as our burden to bear. By instead trusting that we are taken care of, or that we have a connection to all that is, we can lighten our own loads.

This can be especially tough on the perfectionist parts of our SMALL selves. Working with executive women and in my own experience, I have found that being in control is part of what makes us feel safe. Trusting that God or the Universe has our backs and that we don't have to micromanage everything can be uncomfortable. We sometimes feel like if life isn't a struggle, and we aren't stressed out, that we aren't doing it right, or doing enough. In reality, controlling every detail to try to force the outcome we think will make us happy leads to stress and exhaustion, not happiness.

The bottom line here is that you have to have faith. There is nothing that takes away the "I'm not good enough" or "I'm not worthy" conversation like a connection to a loving higher power. For those of you that already have a God or pray to the Universe this may be easier for you. For the rest of you, this is exactly why I created the acronym SELF. If you connect to the energy that is your SELF, your Spiritually Evolved Loving Friend, you have a way to know that you are not alone.

Brené Brown defines faith so eloquently in her book, *The Gifts of Imperfection*. In her research into resilient, wholehearted people, she finds faith, regardless of a person's religious beliefs, to be a defining characteristic. She says, "Faith is a place of mystery where we find the courage to believe in what we cannot see and the strength to let go of our fear of uncertainty."

My point is that ultimately, being a human being can really suck sometimes. When we get all caught up in trying to force things to happen or trying to just make it through another day of having SMALL being really loud. Being able to turn it over is a powerful tool.

Flexing your muscle around letting go could look like memorizing a prayer. It could be a ritual like writing a letter and then burning it. The goal is to shift your thoughts from obsessing about what you are trying to accomplish, or an issue occupying your mind to thoughts about your higher power, or things that lift you up and have you know that you are going to be okay no matter what.

When my friend Pam Grout was on a beach vacation and had just completed her book, *E Squared*, she wrote in the sand,

"E-Squared will become a number one bestseller" and she watched as the waves took that writing out in to the sea. It was her way of letting it go. In case you didn't know, *E Squared* sat on the number one bestseller list in self-help for 21 weeks.

Step seven is an essential step. Sometimes you have to turn it over every hour. I have had experiences that I couldn't stop thinking about and I started turning it over every 15 minutes. Letting go gives you the opportunity to relax and know that all is well in this moment and you don't have to control everything.

CHAPTER 4

The Six Areas of Life

The next section of the book is about applying the steps to your life. In my seminars, I have each participant pick just one area of life to focus on in our session. I will give an overview of the areas, and some things to think about when you consider your own life. Keep focus on loving your SELF first, then go through each area in a detailed way.

Health and well being: One of the most important things in the world is taking care of your physical self. When you take time to work out, take time to enrich yourself, take time to take care of your being and love yourself, you will create more time because you will have more energy. Our bodies send pain and fatigue signals that we sometimes ignore. Body image issues and "shoulds" around diet and exercise abound. The first work many of us need to do in this area is to learn to love and be grateful for the body and health that we have.

Each person, has a different formula for managing their own wellbeing. I, for example, am sugar sensitive. Therefore if I want to manage my emotional wellbeing I can't be overdosing on sugar all the time. If I eat a pie every day, I act like a jerk. I cannot manage my emotions very well. Therefore, it is my responsibility to manage my sugar intake. Notice for yourself how different foods make you feel. Are you giving yourself heartburn? High blood pressure? Low energy? How would your SELF feed the body it lives in?

Each of us must determine for ourselves what works for our body and what doesn't work for our body. I know exercise to be a powerful practice. It gives the brain good juice and is a part of the natural cure for depression. It develops those endorphins that give you that happy feeling that has you be able to maintain your life in a more powerful way. You don't have to run a marathon. You don't have to work out six days a week. Just do something - preferably something you enjoy. Try on the perspective that exercise is a gift to your body and brain.

For some people, the thing to work on in health and well-being is a chronic illness. In that case, there may be work to be done on how you think and speak about that illness. Are you perpetually a victim of your health or body? Is there something else possible for your life if you shift your BS about your condition?

Health and well-being is about what you put into your body and what you need for your body. Get yourself checked out regularly. Do all the stuff you need to do to maintain your health and well-being. Treat your physical body lovingly.

Massage, acupuncture, rest, and taking deep full breaths are gifts to your physical being that can help energize, revitalize, calm, and restore your physical self. Caring for your physical self helps you to create from a strong foundation.

Relationships: If you are going to take on transforming something in the area of relationships, I invite you to select a specific person with whom you want your relationship to grow or improve. Whether it is your mother, spouse, coworker, child, or future partner, the key is remembering that you are not changing a thing about them. They are fine. The way they are is the way they are. You will be exploring your BS (Belief System) and how that impacts your experience of the relationship.

If you have someone that is a challenge in your life, they are your best teacher. You have manifested that person in your life so that you can learn something. They help you see what you are resisting. They help you pay attention to where your focus is.

We all know the woman who keeps dating the same guy with different pants, or has the same complaint about her boss no matter how many she has had. This is because she never learned her lesson from the first time. Lessons show up over and over again in different people until we actually get it.

Sometimes it doesn't feel good. Sometimes I've really got to look at myself and discover what is it in me that is showing up over there that has me confronted. Looking at ourselves is one of the most confronting things we can deal with, and other people are our mirrors. Our experience of the words and behaviors of others are a product of our judgment of the words and behaviors, not the words and behaviors themselves.

Often when I am having a conflict in a relationship, it's about me wanting that person to be different. I think I know how they should be. They didn't get my script for the day. So I flex my muscle around accepting people the way they are. I also have to give up that I already know how they are, or how they will respond if I want to allow for a change in the relationship.

Once we have been in a relationship with someone, we log in to our brains how that person is. We note and begin to anticipate what they say and how they act. We assume they will always act and speak exactly as they have in the past. Without realizing it, we begin reacting to our assumptions rather than actually communicating.

Here is an example from one of my clients. In my seminar she said the words, "*I keep all people at arms distance. Including my husband.*" Once I started asking her questions and coaching her she realized that she had already made up her mind about how her husband would respond to any attempt to talk to him about important things. She got clear that in the past she had been approaching him from that distant place. In our interaction she saw an opening to be able to be vulnerable with her husband. The prospect scared her, but she was willing to try it.

The next morning I got this note from her in my inbox:

Jay,

I would like to thank you for an amazing seminar yesterday. I learned a lot about myself, both in my personal life and business life. I went into this seminar with the assumption that I would only gain business insight but I gained so much more from you yesterday.

Last night I sat down and talked to my husband, really talked and was completely honest. It was very liberating to be honest and to tell him some things I haven't told him, and to tell him my thoughts, feelings and emotions. He was amazing and handled everything I said with the grace of a man who truly loves me.

I am looking forward to the second seminar and maybe working with you in the future.

Have a wonderful day!

She created the beginning of a whole new relationship with her husband. First she had to give up that she already knew how he was going to respond, and be willing to look at how she had been approaching him in the past.

What is it like for the people in your life to have you as their partner?

Finances: When I say that everything is energy, I do mean everything. I'll be the first to tell you that when it comes to money, it's easy to forget that. We give money a lot of power in this world. Certainly without it, food and shelter are harder to come by. Some of us equate our self-worth with how much of it we have. Many of us fear not having enough. The reality is, we (people) made it up as a medium of exchange. We respond emotionally to pieces of paper or numbers on a screen. This is an opportunity to explore the underlying beliefs (again with the BS) that trigger the emotional responses.

Your perceptions and beliefs have money show up in your life the way it does. You have to create new beliefs around money to make big shifts. Everything your parents dealt with around money, you inherited. Many of us, for example, were raised by depression era parents. My dad used to have a saying that was, *"It's not how much money you make, it's how much you don't spend."* That's something I took with me my whole life. All of us have those statements. If you go read Suze Orman, one of the first things she does when she works with people is she has them identify the sayings and conversations their parents had about money. You can start to look at those beliefs that are underneath everything you know about money.

Money is another area where if you can't imagine it, you can't have it. So that's why I want you to pay attention to what you say about money. If you say, "I can't imagine spending that much money on a car." Well, then guess what? You won't be driving that car. You can't wrap your head around it. If you can't stand rich people, you're never going to be one. The energy you put out about money is what comes back at you. That includes everything you say about it and think about it. Whatever you believe about it is what comes back to you around money.

Money is the most triggering point I've ever seen. If you were raised in poverty it can be a very painful experience to untangle your beliefs about money and get to a place where you can really own that you are the one creating your life. Even around money. You must be gentle and kind with yourself while you learn to increase your prosperity consciousness so you can create financial well-being.

One client I worked with on the area of finances knew she was in debt, but she didn't really know how much she owed or to whom. There's no way that you can expect your money to be flowing in a positive way if you don't even know what debts you have. So the first thing we had to do was to get her in integrity with her money. Even if she had to create a payment plan of $5 per month to start paying back all the services in the past that she'd received. Now, a year later, she is completely out of debt. She never thought that being out of debt was even possible a year ago. It turned out she didn't even owe as much as she thought once she sat down to look at it. Often when something scares us, we respond by going numb or into denial. We don't want to know about it. Once she gave up her belief that it wasn't possible, she found that not only was it possible, but things weren't even as bad as she had believed they were.

I highly recommend tithing as a powerful tool to transform your relationship with money. What I mean is giving 10% of your income away to whatever spiritually feeds you. The first time I wrote a tithe check I almost choked. I couldn't even believe I was just giving away that much money. I transformed my relationship to money from the belief that I might not have enough if I gave it away to the more I give the more I have. The amount of that first monthly check quickly became the amount of a weekly check.

These are a few of my favorite books on prosperity consciousness:

Spiritual Economics, by Eric Butterworth
Four Spiritual Laws of Prosperity, by Edwene Gaines
The Soul of Money, by Lynne Twist

Career/Creativity: I want for you to do what you love. When we love what we do, that's evidenced in everything else in our lives. Some of us have a job that pays the bills and do other things to express ourselves creatively. For others, our creative expression is our job. Either way, time and how you spend is it how you expend your energy. If you aren't currently doing anything you love, this is an area to address.

If, currently in your life you are doing a job that you don't enjoy, then I invite you to consider transforming that area of your life. That could mean changing jobs, but it could also mean shifting your perspective (BS) about your current job. You spend at least 40 hours a week doing your job. Many of you work more than that, right? When your job is a constant complaint, that is a lot of energy going in a negative direction.

I have coached a lot of people through the shift from a job to becoming entrepreneurs. I have also coached people who chose to get invested in their jobs and create from within them. These people chose to approach their work from a place of curiosity and service and found a new level of fulfillment. You can create a career or find a way to spend your energy doing something that feels good. That's what I want for you.

My favorite question to ask a client or prospective client is, "What would you do if you knew you couldn't fail?"

The joy and stories I have as a result of asking that question over the last ten years is indescribable. It's part of what makes me know that I am in the right business. I love getting to ask people and see the look on their faces when there really is something inside them they want to do, but up until that moment they have kept it a secret.

One of my favorite success stories around this was a little bittersweet. On one hand the outcome of this question was the beginning of exactly what would make this individual's heart sing. On the other it was the loss of a creative director for my biggest corporate client.

I always let my corporate clients know that my commitment is to their employees' happiness, and that sometimes that means an employee may become clear that they don't want to stay. Often employees are incredibly grateful to work for companies that invest in them in this way and relationships are strengthened. The CEOs I work with understand though that an employee who doesn't really want to be working for them is not in their best interest, but no one wants to lose talented employees. This was a difficult situation to navigate.

After six months of working with this individual we had transformed her stress level, communication, and working relationships. She had done incredible work. As our time working together was nearing an end, I asked that question: "What would you do if you couldn't fail?" She immediately answered, "I would open my own business with my sister."

Wow!

Once she said it out loud she created a new future. As we explored what that would look like, her mind began moving fast. Her excitement and energy were palpable. It was clear in that moment that this was going to happen. I am fortunate to get to be the guy who is there at that moment when a new future is created, and then get to support and coach the baby steps to fruition.

Within six months, she and her sister were so successful they had to hire help. Her former boss handled it with grace and they still collaborate on projects. This is what is possible in a world where people are committed to being their higher self in business.

Anything is possible. If your job isn't a source of joy, transform that area of your life. You want your work to breathe life in to you, not suck it out.

Environment: What I mean about environment is the space in which you live and work. Start with your house, your bedroom, your work space then go out to your community, your neighborhood, and the world. Really look at your surroundings and how you relate to them. Do they reflect the life you want to have? Are you ignoring or putting up with things that truly don't serve you?

Your space reflects and reinforces your energy. Do your shoulders slump when you see the stack of paperwork on your desk? Do you smile when you walk in and notice a photo of a great family trip? Most of us are familiar with the TV show "Hoarders" and the extreme ways environment can reflect fear, but may not be as tuned in to how our environments impact our energy flow in less obvious ways.

If energy is not moving in your life, when you have a "stuck" feeling, move your stuff. Literally, clean out your closet. If you have areas of your life that have been stacked up and stagnant, that is stagnant energy, not moving. You need to move that energy. It makes perfect sense that if everything is energy that cleaning out spaces and moving energy will start creation.

Clean out your life on a regular basis and put things back in to circulation, it is part of the energy flow that you can be very deliberate about. What you give out you get back everywhere in your life. You can look at your environment as the playground as well as the foundation for your energetic flow. It's worth considering what you are giving out and where you want to be purposeful with your energy.

I recently had a seminar participant rid her closet of all the clothes that didn't fit her and that she didn't love. Holding onto several sizes reinforced the body image and self-love issues she has been working to transform. Holding on to the clothes she never wore but that were staring her in the face every day kept those negative thoughts and feelings front and center.

Spirituality: This book is called *Lean Inside* because of the power available in finding the place where you can experience your connection to everything else. Once you experience that connection, there is a knowing and an experience of being known that is hard to describe. Leaning inside has you know that all is well, regardless of any external circumstances. Spirituality is where it's at.

Earlier I introduced you to your SELF. Your SELF is that part of you that is connected to All There Is. Many people have a spiritual or religious understanding of this concept, but it is for atheists and agnostics, too. When you develop spiritual awareness, you will have access peace and contentment. Your life will take on a flow you may never have experienced before.

The first practice where I would make a bold request that you start immediately is meditation. I consider meditation a spiritual practice. However, the documented benefits to health and wellbeing exceed the spirit. There is a multitude of research these days on the benefits of meditation on the brain and on emotional intelligence.

In their book, *How God Changes Your Brain*, neuroscientists Dr. Andrew Newberg and Dr. Mark Waldman report the measurable effect on the brain brought about by spiritual practices. These included meditation and religious rituals. What they came up with were the following findings:

1. Each part of the brain constructs a different perception of God.

2. Every human brain assembles its perceptions of God uniquely, thus giving God different qualities of meaning and value.

3. Spiritual practices, even when stripped of religious beliefs, enhance neural functioning of the brain in ways that improve physical and emotional health.

4. Intense long-term contemplation of God and other spiritual values appears to permanently change the

structure of the parts of the brain that control our moods, give rise to our conscious notions of self, and shape our sensory perceptions of the world.

Isn't that amazing? Permanently change! This is what I'm talking about when I'm talking about retraining your brain. The best way you can retrain your brain is to develop spiritual practices. Contemplative practices strengthen a neurological circuit that generates peacefulness, social awareness, and compassion for others. If I could leave you with one thing it would be this. The more time and energy that you invest in feeding your spirit, the more everything else will fall in to place.

Getting complete with Jesus: For many of you, what is in the way of having a rich spiritual life is your past. It is important for you to get complete with your faith of origin, or any negative association with religions that impact your perception of spirituality. What that means is to get to a place of real forgiveness for your past negative experiences of doctrine or people representing your faith of origin. Many people experience religion as something shoved down their throat and want to avoid anything at all associated with that experience. For some atheists, any suggestion of spiritual practice is too "woo woo" to be taken seriously.

I was raised catholic. Part of the reason I tried to kill myself was because I believed that I was going to go to hell for being gay. I was also taught and believed that killing yourself was a mortal sin. Therefore, if I killed myself I was also going to go to hell. I figured I would just get there faster and then my family wouldn't have to deal with the shame of me being gay. I was told by a priest when I was 18 years old that I could be gay, I just couldn't practice homosexuality. If I did, I was not welcome to take communion. This experience fueled my anger and righteous indignation toward the church. It allowed me to judge and assess anyone that was religious in any way.

Through AA, I developed an understanding of the difference between spirituality and religion. However, I still had a chip on my shoulder regarding Christianity, my faith of origin. Many years later I was welcomed as a transgender person at Dumbarton United Methodist Church with open arms. I was told that I was loved and shown a different version of Jesus. I got to stop making my entire understanding of a religion and religious figure be about past negative experiences. I was able to heal my past hurts around religion. What freedom.

I don't consider myself a Christian now. I do consider Jesus as a powerful example of love and forgiveness. He is one of my teachers.

I know a lot of people, especially gay people, who have been really hurt by religion. If you are someone that has been hurt or had religion shoved down your throat, I hope you will take the time to start untangling your stories around it. Give yourself space to take baby steps and be gentle with your SELF. It will provide you with great peace to get complete. You may find that it aides you in connecting to and creating a whole new appreciation for your SELF.

CHAPTER 5

Practical Application

Now we will walk through the 7 steps so you can see how it works. These are the exercises we do in my live seminar. If you practice and do this work and you don't quit, it will make a difference.

Strap yourself in. Here we go.

Pick either an area of life that we listed above or choose anything in your life that you want to transform or make different.

Step 1: Commit

Will you commit to your own transformation by practicing progress NOT perfection in this area?

If No, accept that you like this area the way it is. The payoff for having it this way is too good to give up. Stop complaining about it. You love it.

If Yes, write a note from your highest SELF with a promise to stop beating yourself up in this area. In the letter, commit to give up perfectionism by practicing constant forgiveness of yourself and others on this journey.

Date the letter from your SELF and put it some place where you can find it later when you need a reminder.

Step 2: Get to a happy place by owning all of it

Take out your journal or a piece of paper and write down the area or name of your topic.

Set a timer. I recommend about ten minutes.

Now write.

Write out everything you think about this area of your life. Write out everything you can recall speaking about this area of your life. Write what you say to yourself about it and what you say to others. Write until the timer goes off, or until you can't think of another thing.

Go back now and read it through at least three times.

Circle or highlight key phrases that are familiar. Particularly look for things you know you say out loud. For example: "I don't know what I want", "It's all on me", "I don't understand", "I am not _____ enough", "I don't have enough _____".
Notice your feelings and energy as you think about the area.

Give yourself as clear a picture as you can about how that area of your life is right now. Mill around in it as long as you like. (In seminar they only get five minutes.)

NOTE: You might consider that this area of your life is like a knot in a shoe string. It is tight and difficult to grasp, to loosen, or give air to. Try to get a clear picture of all the mess and drama without judging or being defensive. Like pulling blindly at a big knot, your judgments won't fix it, but may just pull it tighter. All the questions below are designed to start to loosen the knot. Each person will resonate with a different question depending on where you are on your own journey of being able to own your own created world. Be patient with yourself. These questions are designed to move everyone at some level.

OK. Now Stand up.

Take a few deep breaths and shake out your body like you are shaking something off of you. You might dance around for a minute.

Write out your answers to each question below. If one calls to you, spend time there. If you feel resistance to answering one of the questions, that may be one to focus on. Take on the resistance by being kind to yourself and being curious. Let go of defensiveness and perfectionism as you answer the questions. These are your answers to help you identify what has you producing the current results you have in your life. Remember that nothing is wrong.

This area of your life: _____

Why did you create it this way?

Who are you making wrong?

What do you get to be right about?

Do you get to be a victim?

Do you get to be a martyr?

Are you being right that you can't or aren't good enough?

Having your life this way: Does it get you out of being powerful?

Does it prove you are not worthy?

Who do you need to forgive?

What story from the past is there to reframe or create a new meaning around?

What lesson did you learn in the past that has you create your life this way now?

This can be an ongoing process as you practice being 100% response able for your life. You will continue to make progress and deepen this conversation.

By now you are probably getting a pretty clear picture of this area of your life. Look at the story it tells. If you cannot own that you have a hand in creating it, at least you can see that this is your perception or the lens through which you view this area of your life. You start to see your beliefs and can identify the future you've sentenced yourself to. You will always be _____. You will never be _____. Notice the sentence you pass and the reality or future you are affirming with your thoughts and words. Is it what you want?

I invite you consider that you did create it, and you created it this way because in some way it served or supported your BS (Belief System). My want for you is to start to shift from this being the Truth of your life to just a view that can be shifted so that something else is possible. What if you consciously guided your thoughts?

This is why our goal from here on out is to NEVER speak the words you circled or highlighted again as long as you live. It will take practice, and you must STOP speaking all that stuff you wrote down. You must STOP speaking it. Go online and look up Bob Newhart's "stop it" sketch. It's silly, but sage advice. STOP IT.

Are you ready to give up your old story?

Are you ready to create something else?

If No, keep working on it. For some of you it will be scary to give up having this area of your life in chaos. Being at the effect rather than the cause of situations in our lives is comfortable and familiar.

If Yes, we are ready to move to Step 3.

NOTE: At this point you are also to be engaged in making your own happiness a priority. Work through the Happiness and Productivity Workout as it is an ongoing workout. You can take a new area every month if you like.

Step 3: Get clear about what you want and ASK for it.

Now that you are ready to give up how it has been in this area of your life, it's time to purposely create how we want it to be.

Start by getting clear about what you want in this area.

What do you want?

If you could have anything in this area what would it be?

My favorite question: What would you do if you knew you couldn't fail?

NOTE: Immediately you may think that the answer to these questions will be things like, "more time", "more organized"... Answers that start with you judging yourself (or others, or fixed circumstances like hours in the day) are more of the same story. You are aiming to create a vision of what you want, free from your old story. Go back to Steps 1 and 2 and keep working to own it without making yourself wrong if you find yourself stuck in just trying to fix yourself, or the area you described in Step 2.

Write down what you want, even if you can't completely see it yet. Write down and articulate what you can see. Start creating a new vision and a new conversation. Don't get bogged down in perfectionism. This is your vision to continue to hone.

ASK: Say a prayer, if you pray. If you don't, say it out loud to the universe or a tree. I don't care who you ask. Just ask for what you want. Be as specific as possible. Write it down. Collage, create art, or sing a song about it. Ask the person who can give you what you want.

Step 4: Baby step it out

Now that you know what you want, you should be able to see a few steps you can take in that direction. There has to be a beginning, you have to take a first step. My seminar participants always leave with a first step of scheduling something in their calendars.

Start there. Schedule something. It could be a manicure, a doctor's appointment, a trip to the gym, a call to an expert.

Just schedule something and you have already taken your first baby step action.

Now that you are in action, you have to create a new conversation for your life around this area. If you do not shift your thinking and speaking in this area you will go back to it. You cannot keep speaking the old conversation you wrote down in Step 2. Instead, you must speak and think something new.

For further resources on how to shift to affirmative thinking and speaking, I recommend *The Intenders Handbook*, by Tony Burroughs, *The Game of Life and How to Play It* by Florence Scovel Shinn, *What to Say When You Talk to Your Self* by Shad Helmstetter.

As I've said, the mistake people make with affirmations is trying to speak affirmations that their BS (Belief System) or operating system doesn't agree with or believe. When you try to go from saying I hate myself to I love myself, the brain won't be fooled. Instead, all the habitual thoughts are triggered.

This is where the baby step or Bridge Affirmations come into play. Start with words and phrases that we can say and believe. By speaking them we get in to action retraining our brains and support the success of our baby step actions. These baby steps create clarity and illuminate the path. Action provides clarity.

Let's use the example or area of self love.

We've committed to progress not perfection, and we are willing to release and keep releasing the past through forgiveness. We commit to give up speaking the way we have in the past, which affirmed negativity and self abuse.

The endgame affirmation is to be able to say, "I love my self" and not gag or throw up a little. Ultimately I want for you to know and feel that it is true for you. Initially, you can't speak "I love myself" without having your BS meter go off. It causes you to roll your eyes at the least, if not go off on a mental tirade of why it isn't true, you don't deserve for it to be true, and why you are an idiot for even thinking it.

We start then with our first bridge affirmation.

Something like: "I'm willing to be open to the idea that I could love my self".

Say this for a few weeks while you get into action just doing a few things to nurture your self. Schedule a massage or a pedicure. Buy yourself that pair of boots you have been wanting. Set aside time to do things you enjoy.

Once you have done these things, your last affirmation is starting to seem weak. By now you can say in earnest, "I do things that nurture my self".

Keep taking the baby step actions toward your very specific goal.

Take on doing a compassion meditation. Start walking with a friend at lunch.

By now it is not only true that you do things that nurture your self, you can also say in earnest "I am learning to love my self".

Write this down and say it as often as possible. Align the rest of your language around this and start to notice when you speak and think of yourself in unloving or mean ways.

Keep taking baby step actions – commit to only talking to your self like you would a good friend. Start meditating every day for ten minutes. Stay in action around your goals. Take on the Happiness and Productivity Workout and start getting things in integrity.

Now you are starting to experience real power. Your life is clearly of your own design. Now you can say in all honesty:

"I am committed to facing head on anything in the way of loving my self."

Stay in action. Take on a service project. Keep taking on your integrity. You may have some down days, but keep being willing to be vulnerable and not quit.

This is how to move from baby step affirmations to endgame affirmations. This is how to use baby step actions to fulfill on the vision you hold for your life.

Step 5: Put in accountability like crazy

Ask friends to remind you that you have committed to this path. Seek out a counselor or mentor or coach to pay to hold you accountable. Attend classes where your attendance is documented.

In seminar each woman leaves with an accountability buddy or team.

Step 6. *Imagine it*

Spend time envisioning and imagining how your life will look when your endgame affirmation doesn't set off your BS meter.

Step 7: *Let it go*

Make a practice of turning it over any and every time you feel resistance, notice yourself trying to force an outcome, or worrying.

You have a big breakthrough because you are finally ready to see that you are the one creating your life exactly as it is all the time. That is when you can honestly say,

I love my self.

Mission Accomplished!

You can apply these steps to any area of your life. Some areas will take six weeks some will take a lifetime. There will always be more to learn about yourself and more to create in your life. This is about training yourself to be able to own everything without being defensive. I want you to be able to look at all of it and say with curiosity, not judgement, "Why did I create it this way?"

EXAMPLES

I'm going to walk you through two examples from the areas we listed above to deepen your grasp on how it works. These examples are fictional, however they resemble work I do with my clients. We will look at weight loss and finances as these are two popular topics. Please know that I am only writing enough for you to get the gist. When you do this work, you need to be prepared to dig in. Really tell the whole story, uncover the things you think and believe about yourself, and get willing to forgive. The only way to really ensure a new future is to complete the past.

Health and Well Being:

Name: Oprah Sesame
Area: Weight Loss

Step 1: Commit

I, Oprah Sesame, on this date, March 7th, 2015, commit to Progress not Perfection in this area of my life. I promise to give up being mean to me, or beating myself up around the area of weight loss. I commit to speaking to myself the way I would a good friend.

> *Dear Oprah,*
>
> *This is a vulnerable issue for you. It's time to be kind to you. You can do this. It is time to stop playing SMALL. I have great faith that together we can do this. Thank you for being willing to practice progress not perfection. Let's give up beating up on us. It doesn't serve you. You are a powerful woman and accomplishing this goal will be the one thing that makes the biggest difference in your ability to serve the world.*
>
> *I love you,*
> *Your SELF*

Step: 2 Get happy by owning it all

Exercise: Write it out. Getting to a limiting belief, uncovering the story.

Weight Loss by Oprah Sesame.

> *I have been fat my whole life, or at least I thought I was fat when I was a kid. Now I look back and realize that I wasn't fat then, I only thought I was, but I'm fat now. I have tried every diet in the world. I can't lose weight. I lose weight and then I gain it back all the time. I am fat. Weight loss is an uphill battle. I feel powerless to change it. I am powerless. I can't make a difference. I don't have time to work out. I have so much to do. I'm the only one. If I don't do it no one will. It's all on me. I am exhausted.*

NOTE: Can you feel the energy of this? It is heavy. The weight of the world is on her shoulders.

Circle or highlight words:

> *I have been fat my whole life, or at least I thought I was fat when I was a kid. Now I look back and realize that I wasn't fat then, I only thought I was, but I'm fat now. I have tried every diet in the world. I <u>can't</u> lose weight. I lose weight and then I gain it back all the time. <u>I am fat.</u> <u>Weight loss is an uphill battle.</u> I feel powerless to change it. <u>I</u>*

am powerless. I can't make a difference. I don't have time to work out. I have so much to do. I'm the only one. If I don't do it no one will. It's all on me. I am exhausted.

Your sentence: It's all on me.
Your current affirmations: I am fat, I am powerless, I can't, I am exhausted.

These highlighted words are now your **watch words.** These are words to watch out for in your own speaking. You're going to commit to never speaking or thinking this way again, but it doesn't happen overnight. This has been your conversation for a long time. It will take time to let it go completely. You practice by noticing your watch words and consciously choosing different ones.

NOTE: Any phrase that starts with "I am" is an affirmation, and some believe a command to the universe.

Commit to stop it.

I, Oprah Sesame, declare that I will stop speaking the above conversation about weight loss. I will practice affirming only my new vision for my life in this area. I am willing to transform this area of my life and have it be different. I give that old conversation and thoughts no power.

Step 3: Get clear about what you want and ask

Oprah wants to lose weight. She is not losing weight to gain confidence or love, though she has collapsed those goals in the past. She asks the question, "What will my life be like when I lose the weight?" Her answer is that she will have the energy and ability to keep up with her children and grandchildren, and enjoy a long life. She will be an inspiring example to her son and granddaughter.

Once you get clear about the want then you ask.

Oprah: I ask for the courage and tenacity to keep on the path toward an energetic and healthy physical body.

Step 4. Baby step it out

Remember we start by putting something in the calendar to schedule. In this case, Oprah puts in her calendar that she will sign up for a weight loss support program. Oprah is already in action and creating an accountability structure.

Her Endgame Affirmation is: I love my body and am grateful for my health and vitality.

Baby Steps.

Bridge Affirmation: I am willing to start taking steps towards health and vitality.

Actions: Start working on forgiveness for me and my past around weight loss. Start walking 3x per week. (Asks a friend to join her to create accountability.)

A few months later:

Bridge Affirmation: I am starting to see that I can be healthy and vital and I treat my body well.

Actions: Continue to track food and activity through weight loss support program. Reframe an old story about myself from high school.

A few months later: (13 pounds down and feeling good).

Bridge Affirmation: I am on a path of health and vitality. I am starting to appreciate my body.

Action: Join a gym and work with a personal trainer.

All the time she is moving forward with her baby steps, she is continuing to work the other six steps. She is putting in accountability, visioning her success, and letting go of the outcome. She is revisiting her commitment, and being grateful for successes and forgiving of her shortfalls. Her focus is on progress not perfection.

Finances

Name: Joyce Grace
Area: Finances – Getting out of debt

Step 1: Commit

I, Joyce Grace, on this date, May 7th, 2017, commit to progress not perfection in this area of my life. I promise to give up being mean to me or beating myself up around the area of debt. I commit to speaking to myself the way I would a good friend.

> *Dear Joyce,*
>
> *This is a vulnerable issue for you. It's time to be kind to you. You can do this. It is time to stop playing SMALL. I have great faith that together we can do this. Thank you for being willing to practice progress not perfection. Let's give up beating up on US. It doesn't serve you. You are a powerful woman and accomplishing this goal will be the one thing that makes the biggest difference in your ability to serve the world.*
>
> *I love you,*
> *Your SELF*

Step: 2 Get happy by owning it all

Exercise: Write it out. Getting to a limiting belief, uncovering the story.

Debt by Joyce Grace:

> *I can't get a handle on my finances. I have debt, but I don't know how much really. I fear opening the mail or getting phone calls. Just when I think I'm going to get ahead something happens and I'm broke again. I don't have any money. I am broke. I haven't got two nickels to rub together. I'm too poor to pay attention. I barely have enough to get by, but I always get by. I don't have the money to create something new. I can't see my way out of this. I can't afford it. I'll never get out of debt.*

NOTE: This is classic poverty or lack mentality. Notice where the focus is. It's on the debt and lack rather than on prosperity and creating wealth.

Circle or highlight words

> *<u>I can't get a handle on my finances</u>. I have debt, but I don't know how much really. I fear opening the mail or getting phone calls. Just when I think I'm going to get ahead something happens and I'm broke again. <u>I don't have any money</u>. <u>I am broke</u>. I haven't got two nickels to rub together.*

I'm too poor to pay attention. <u>I barely have enough</u> to get by, but <u>I always get by</u>. I don't have the money to create something new. I can't see my way out of this. I can't afford it. <u>I'll never get out of debt</u>.

Your sentence: I'll never get out of debt.

Your current affirmations: I am broke, I don't have any money, I can't get ahead.

These highlighted words are now your **watch words.** Words to watch out for in your own speaking. You are going to commit to never speaking or thinking this way again but it doesn't happen overnight. This has been your conversation for a long time. It will take time to let it go completely. You practice by noticing your watch words.

NOTE: Any phrase that starts with "I AM" is an affirmation and some believe a command to the universe to fulfill on it.

Next, commit to letting it go.

I, Joyce Grace, declare that I will stop speaking the above conversation about my finances. I will practice affirming only my new vision for my life in this area. I am willing to transform this area of my life and have it be different. I give it up.

Step 3: Get clear about what you want and ask

Joyce's goal is to get out of debt. She asks the question: What will my life be like when I am debt free? She will have the peace of mind that she can pay her bills and start to build wealth. She will know herself as capable of creating prosperity.

Now that she has that clarity, she asks.

Joyce: I ask for peace and prosperity for the greater good of all concerned.

Step 4. Baby step it out

Remember we start by putting something in your calendar to schedule. In this case, Joyce puts in her calendar time to go through the debt and get clear about to whom she owes money, and how much. This puts Joyce already in action.

End Game Affirmation: I am prosperous and free.

Baby Steps.

Bridge Affirmation: I am willing to start taking steps toward prosperity.

Actions: Start working on forgiveness for me and my past around finances. Write out conversations my parents handed me about money. Create a spread sheet of who I owe and how much. Start making payments even if they are really small.

A few months later: (Debt organized and starting to have clarity).

Bridge Affirmation: I am paying off my debt. I am starting to see a path toward prosperity.

Actions: Continue to pay down debt. Set up automatic payment plan through bank (accountability structure!) Read books on prosperity consciousness and money management. Open a savings account.

A few months later: Debt reduction plan made, showing her out of debt in 18 months.

Bridge Affirmation: I am on a path of peace and prosperity.

Action: Keep paying down debt. Start giving away just a little money every paycheck to something that spiritually lifts me up. Buy the new purse because I want it and can afford it, instead of because my old one fell apart.

Keeping her focus on progress not perfection in this area, Joyce Grace continues to work the 7 steps. She hones her vision, let's go of attachment, and gives thanks for her continued progress. Any time she stumbles on her path or discovers a new story to be reframed, she approaches it with forgiveness and love.

THE FINAL CHAPTER

My goal for this book is for it to be short and practical. I have a lot of half-read personal development books on my shelf and I know many others that do also.

It's important to remember that your brain and your operating system take in information and file it away. If you do not stay conscious, you will always revert to old behavior and old ways of thinking, feeling, and speaking. I have given you one formula that works and hopefully I've made you curious enough to keep learning. What are we here for if not to continue to grow and change as humans? So much amazing research is coming out every day on how our brains and human systems operate. I invite you to keep reading and listening and watching and pulling toward you all that feeds your mind body and soul.

One of my biggest commitments is the practical part. I want you to be left with an easy to follow formula.

That being said, if you do nothing but start with the following practices, it will make a difference:

1. Practice Gratitude: Give thanks for all things, even the bad stuff.
2. Practice Kindness: Be kind to yourself and others.
3. Practice Forgiveness: Constantly forgive yourself and others.
4. Practice Mindfulness: Practice keeping your mind in this moment instead of the past or an invented future.

The key to truly being happy and fulfilled is not anything out there. It's an inside job.

Healing the inside means really killing off, once and for all, the conversation of I'm not worthy. I'm not good enough.

My greatest wish is that this book gives you access to that.

I see the divinity in you.